HYMNS AND HYMN SINGING

Also by David Baker
THE ORGAN (Shire Publications 1991, revised edition 1993)

HYMNS
AND
HYMN SINGING
A POPULAR GUIDE

by
DAVID BAKER
and
JOAN WELSBY

The Canterbury Press
Norwich

© David Baker and Joan Welsby 1993

First published 1993 by The Canterbury Press Norwich
(a publishing imprint of Hymns Ancient & Modern Limited
a registered charity)
St Mary's Works, St Mary's Plain,
Norwich, Norfolk, NR3 3BH

British Library Cataloguing in Publication Data

A catalogue record for this book is available
from the British Library

ISBN 1–85311–068–X

*Typeset by Rowland Phototypesetting Limited,
Bury St Edmunds, Suffolk
and printed in Great Britain by
St Edmundsbury Press Limited,
Bury St Edmunds, Suffolk*

Non vox, sed votum
Non musica chordula, sed cor;
Non clamans, sed amans,
Psallit in aure Dei.

(As quoted in Arthur Bedford's
'The Great Abuse of Musick' (1711)

Address one another in psalms and hymns and
spiritual songs, singing and making melody
to the Lord with all your heart,
always and forever giving thanks

(Philippians 5:18)

ACKNOWLEDGEMENTS

A number of people must be thanked for their help in making this book possible. Kenneth Baker, of The Canterbury Press Norwich, must be thanked for his help and support throughout the project. Gordon Dickson deserves our gratitude for giving of his time to produce his excellent line drawings. A number of colleagues and friends made helpful suggestions as to what should be included in the book and the Glossary in particular. Acknowledgement is due to the University of East Anglia Library, Norwich, for permission to reproduce illustrations from its collections of hymn books, other texts and older journals. Permission to reproduce illustrations was kindly given as follows: Stephen Kaye Photography p. viii; Royal School of Church Music pp. 1, 124; Gordon Dickson pp. 5, 36, 43, 72, 81, 89, 90, 91, 103; Denis Wright p. 13; Hymns Ancient and Modern Ltd pp. 22, 24, 39, 108; The Society of Antiquaries p. 56; The Royal National Institute for the Blind p. 106; Keith Ellis p. 109; Wingfield Arts p. 128; Ron Sherlock p. 110.

Due acknowledgement is also given to the many hymnology collections referred to and included in the Bibliography on pp. 129–130.

CONTENTS

Three Choirs Festival, Worcester Cathedral 1992

INTRODUCTION

ALMOST everyone knows at least one hymn and most people sing a number of hymns during the course of their lives – whether as part of a religious service, a celebration of some kind (Christmas, for example) or at some other major gathering – as for example on the football terraces at Cup Final Day. Some hymns and hymn tunes are known and sung round the world. *Rock of ages*, *O God, our help in ages past* and *Adeste Fideles* are three such hymns.

What is the origin of hymns? Why were they written and for what purpose? What is the story of the most famous hymns? Who were the main hymn writers of their day?

This book sets out to answer these and other questions, giving a history of the hymn from classical times, through the development of the Roman and Orthodox Churches and then to the post-Reformation period, when the great Protestant hymns were written. The story continues with a section on the Wesleys – the great eighteenth-century hymn writers, who wrote many hymns still in regular use today – and their nineteenth-century successors. Reference is made to the great collections of hymns such as *Hymns Ancient and Modern* and *The English Hymnal*.

Most hymn texts (the words) are associated with one particular tune and throughout this book hymn tunes and the context in which they were composed and first used are studied and described. The book includes short histories of some of the most famous tunes in a Glossary, and there is both a Bibliography and a short Discography. The many illustrations depict composers and hymn writers of their day, hymn singing, major centres for hymn composition and performance and famous collections of hymns and hymn tunes.

The subject of hymns and hymn singing is vast and not all of it can be covered in a short guide such as this; we hope that it will nevertheless inform and interest any who wish to know more about the subject.

September 1993   DAVID BAKER
JOAN WELSBY
Wymondham, Norfolk

CHAPTER ONE

What is a Hymn?

Look in most hymn books and one will find the same things. The majority of church congregations sing from words-only editions of their hymn book. This will normally contain between five and six hundred texts, covering all aspects of the ecclesiastical year. The arrangement of the texts will vary from book to book, but will normally group similar texts according to the season – Advent, Christmas, New Year, and so on; special occasion – Wedding, Funeral, Baptism, Saint's Day; time of day (e.g. morning, evening), type of church service (such as Communion or Baptism) or special group (as for example children or societies).

The fuller edition of the hymn book contains music in addition to the words. This may consist of the tune alone (Melody Edition) or may contain full harmonised versions, usually in four vocal parts – soprano, alto, tenor and bass (satb). Some hymn tunes are printed with a separate keyboard accompaniment, whether for piano or organ.

The 1991 winners (Oliver Sammons and Michelle Godfrey) of the Royal School of Church Music's Choirboy and Choirgirl of the Year Competition

1

PASSION CHORALE. (7 6. 7 6. D.)

Melody by H. L. HASSLER, 1564–1612.
Adapted and harmonized by J. S. BACH.

Hymn tune with metre counted out

Most hymn books also have a list of the hymns which they contain, together with various indices – of first lines of texts, of tunes, of metres, of writers of the words and of composers or arrangers of the music. Each hymn is numbered for ease of location.

Each hymn tune and hymn text will be printed to a standard format within the hymn book. While the details will vary from book to book and version to version, most collections of hymns include the same basic information, at least in the full music edition.

Tunes

Take a widely available hymn book such as *Hymns Ancient and Modern Revised*. Open the full music edition at almost any page: there the reader will find the category under which the hymn is classified (as for example,

Christmas or General, or Holy Communion or 'For those at sea'); the hymn number and the name of the hymn tune (such as GOPSAL', REGENT SQUARE, CHRISTCHURCH or GWALCHMAI). These hymn tune names often tell an interesting story. Some are named after places, events or people. Some are called after the composer or the first line of the hymn text to which the tune is normally sung. Others commemorate an important saint or other figure in the church's history. Some tunes are known by more than one name. The tune YORKSHIRE, for example, is also called STOCKPORT in *The English Hymnal*. In S.S. Wesley's *The European Psalmist* (1872), it is called either LEAMINGTON or DORCHESTER! The Glossary at the end of the book lists some of the best known hymn tunes, together with a brief account of their history and gives the reasons for their names, where known and of especial relevance.

Metre

Next to the name of the tune will usually come a note of the metre – L.M. (Long Metre), S.M. (Short Metre), 7777, 7676D – are examples. This denotes the number of syllables in each line and each verse of the hymn text and allows the user to find alternative melodies which will 'fit' the words if the tune printed above the text (the 'set' tune) is not to be used. A hymn text with a metre of '7777', for example, has four lines, each containing seven syllables. Normally, each verse of the hymn repeats this standard pattern. Sometimes the figures will be grouped according to the way in which the writer of the text has grouped the lines of each verse, as for example 88.88.88. or 888.888.

Three metres have particular names. They are: Long Metre (LM) which is in fact 88.88; Short Metre (SM) or 66.86; and Common Metre (CM) – 86.86. CM is also known as Ballad Metre since it was used in many old English ballads. Some hymn texts are 'irregular'; they do not fit any standard pattern and, as a result, both text and music vary in their metre from verse to verse.

Above the music and alongside the name of the tune and its metre will be the name of the composer. Most modern hymn books draw upon a

Margaret — Irregular   T. R. Matthews, 1826–1910

mf Thou didst | leave thy throne and thy | kingly crown,
When thou | camest to earth for me;

An Example of Irregular metre

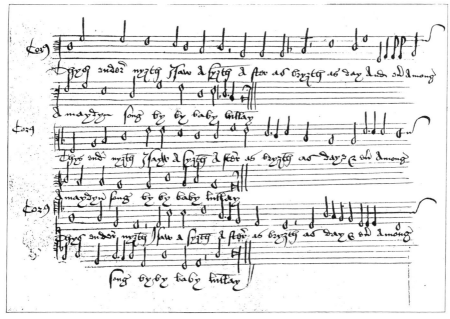

An English Carol of the Sixteenth century
(from Historical Companion to Hymns Ancient & Modern)

wide range of sources for both their tunes and their words and there may be many different composers, countries and ages represented. Modern collections will include the plainsong melodies of the early Christian Church, the chants of the Catholic Church and the great chorales and metrical psalms and hymns of the Protestant Churches of Europe as well as the eighteenth and nineteenth century Anglican and Nonconformist Churches and the churches of North America and other parts of the world. Many tunes are actually folk melodies, not originally intended for use in religious worship.

Carols

'Carols' are also found in hymn books. Normally associated with Christmastide, they use texts which tell the Christmas story in some way. A number of carols tell of Christ's life and Passion. Like other kinds of hymn, carols are normally strophic or verse-repeating. The carol was originally a song to which people danced, perhaps from the Greek *choros*, meaning an outside dance, and also *choraules (one who accompanies the dance)*, or, in its liturgical sense, the word may be a corruption of the Greek *Kyrie eleison*, resulting in the medieval French word 'kyrielle'. The carol soon became part of the Christian Church's music and has remained popular ever since. Certainly by the early fourteenth century, the word as we now know and spell it was being used in Britain. For many years, perhaps because of its secular and out-

4

door connotations it was for many ordinary people the main form of 'congregational' music.

Harmony and Unison

Many present-day hymn books give details concerning the original source of the tune and its harmony. A number of great early collections recur in these references, such as Sternhold and Hopkins, Tate and Brady and Chetham's Psalmody. Some tunes were commissioned by the compilers of these early hymn books and many melodies were written by well-known composers such

Orlando Gibbons

as Orlando Gibbons and John Dowland in the case of seventeenth-century English anthologies.

Some tunes did not originally have any harmony – either because they were folk tunes or because the churches in which they were first sung only allowed unison singing. Some editions of these tunes are especially notable for their harmonisations by later composers, including the elaborate settings of the early Lutheran chorale melodies by the great eighteenth-century German composer Johann Sebastian Bach. Later chapters discuss the development of hymn tunes, the contribution made by different composers and editors and the history of the many hymn books that have been printed from the sixteenth century onwards.

Moving down the page of the hymn book, then comes the music itself. As already noted, a full harmony version

From a page of The Whole Booke of Psalmes by Sternhold & Hopkins, 1594

of a hymn will normally be printed in four parts. The top or soprano part has the tune – the melody sung by the congregation or the general mass of people – the other three parts provide a harmony. In earlier centuries, the melody was in the tenor part (so called because it 'held' the tune – from the Latin *teneo*). Versions of hymns where the tune is in the tenor part are still printed in hymn books, usually as an alternative version to the standard one. Such versions are usually called *Faburden* (French Fauxbourdon), literally meaning 'false bass' from the medieval use of the term, presumably because in older music the tenor line acted as the lowest or bass part. In the Middle Ages, the faburden was an improvised form of harmony whose rules were so well known that the performers could sing it without needing to use written or printed notation.

Some hymns are intended to be sung in *unison*; everybody sings the tune, either unaccompanied, or with an instrumental accompaniment. Some hymns are also printed with a descant. This is a countermelody sung in the treble or soprano part with the congregation or the remainder of the choir singing the hymn melody proper in unison. The singers are accompanied in this case, often with a different harmony. Whether or not there is a descant (often sung to the last verse of the hymn), verses sung in unison are generally provided with alternative and more varied harmonies by the accompanist. In western Christian churches, accompaniment has been provided by a keyboard instrument – mainly the organ – for the last two hundred years, though many other kinds of accompaniment are possible and have been used.

Veni, Creator Spiritus

Hymn set in fauxbourdon   Gilles Binchois (*c.*1400–1460)

An example of faburden

Some hymn texts are printed with more than one tune. Different churches use one in preference to the other depending upon which tune is better known to that group. Some of the tunes have directions concerning their performance; so too do many hymn texts – different lines and verses often have dynamic markings (soft – medium/loud – loud) attached. Some hymn books also suggest which of the verses should be sung in harmony and which in unison. The first and the last verses are often those where everyone sings the tune.

Most hymn texts have at least two verses; some have six or more. The average number of verses is four or five. Many hymn books give performers the option of not singing some verses in order to reduce the length of the hymn in performance. The normal convention is to place an asterisk by those verses which can be omitted if required.

Hymn Sources

The words of hymns vary considerably in their mood and sentiment depending upon the theme. Some depict a particular scene or time from the church's year; others aim to encapsulate a particular feeling or activity – as for example praise or mourning. Most texts rhyme. Many hymns began life as poems before they were ever set to music and can be read effectively rather than being sung. Rhyming texts are easier to remember than blank prose – a distinct advantage in times when most of the congregation could not read. As discussed in later chapters, hymn texts – like hymn tunes – have been

borrowed from one hymn book to another and from one language to another. In the eighteenth and nineteenth centuries, for example, many German chorale texts were translated into English, while in the previous two centuries, it was the Swiss-French versified psalms which, in translation, were the basis of many English-language hymn books.

The author's name is printed at the end of the hymn. Only rarely is the writer of the words the composer of the music. Indeed, some texts are composites of words by different authors, just as the tunes are adaptations from more than one composer's work. As with the tunes, most modern hymn books draw on a wide range of sources for their texts, though there are some famous hymn writers whose work is found in most hymn books – at least in the English-speaking world; people such as the Wesley brothers, Isaac Watts, George Herbert, H. W. Baker, Mrs C. F. Alexander. Their contribution to the development of the hymn is discussed later in this book.

Many hymn texts come from non-Anglican traditions; English-language hymn books contain translations or paraphrases of many Greek, Latin, French, German and other texts from many traditions and centuries. The Old Testament psalms have themselves been turned into a form of hymn generally known as the metrical psalm. Here the text has been paraphrased into a regular verse-repeating metre form so that it can be sung to a simple tune, as with other hymns.

The Song of Triumph.

Christ the LORD is risen again!
Christ hath broken every chain!
Hark, the angels shout for joy,
Singing evermore on high,
                              Hallelujah.

He who gave for us His life,
Who for us endured the strife,
Is our Paschal Lamb to-day!
We too sing for joy, and say:
                              Hallelujah.

He who bore all pain and loss
Comfortless upon the cross,
Lives in glory now on high,
Pleads for us and hears our cry:
                              Hallelujah.

An illustrated Easter Hymn from the 1868 edition of Lyra Germanica published by Longmans, Green, Reader and Dyer

8

One problem sometimes found with hymn texts is the fact that not all the verses fit equally well to the tune to which they are set. In some cases, notes have to be added or subtracted in particular verses – especially where the metre is an irregular one. These notes are usually printed smaller than the rest of the notes in the music editions of hymn books. The best tunes and hymn texts take account of the fact that the words need to be accentuated correctly in order both to emphasise the meaning and the metre. Not all hymns achieve this – even some of the most popular ones.

Amen

At the end of some hymns the reader will find both the word 'Amen' and the two chords of music (the 'Amen' or plagal cadence) which are to be said or sung at the end of the hymn. The word 'Amen' comes from the

An Amen cadence

Hebrew for certainty, truthfulness or faithfulness. Both the Old and New Testaments in the Bible use the word liturgically at the end of some psalms and similar compositions. In some traditions, where the congregation was illiterate or the music complex, 'Amen' was the only part of the hymn or other piece in which those lay people attending the service actually joined. By concluding a hymn with an 'Amen', the congregation affirms what it has been singing about. In

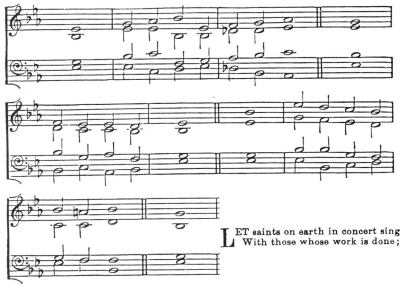

LET saints on earth in concert sing
With those whose work is done;

An example of a metrical psalm tune

9

Festival of Parochial Choirs, Southwell Cathedral (from a drawing by S. Read.

this context, the word is best translated as the phrase 'so be it'. In some churches, an 'Amen' is sung whether or not it is printed in the book.

These, then, are the basic features of the hymn: text, almost invariably grouped into two or more verses in one of a number of standard metric forms and usually rhyming; a tune, with or without three other parts to provide the harmony; an (optional) amen cadence.

Hymns in worship
The word 'hymn' (from the Greek *Hymnos*, meaning a song in praise of gods or heroes) can be defined

10

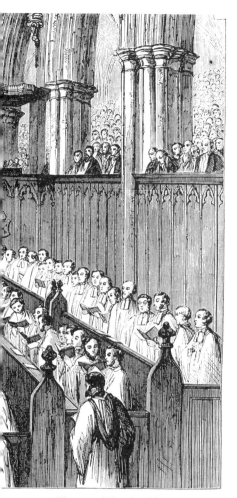

Illustrated London News, 1861)

believers of the particular branch of the faith which collected them.

Most hymns are suitable for use in a religious or liturgical setting – they provide a communal – or even an individual – means of worship. Throughout the history of the hymn, but especially in those ages and countries when and where the vast majority of the congregation could not read, the hymn provided church leaders with a way of instructing the general mass of people in the Faith. Because the texts were easily remembered, so too would the message be communicated to those who sang and learnt hymns. Though the texts can be read, it is in combination with music that hymns are normally performed. The very earliest hymns would be recited or chanted or sung antiphonally, as still happens in churches where responsorial music is sung, with two groups answering each other with alternate verses or half-verses.

There has been almost continual debate about how music written for church worship should be composed and performed. Saint Augustine of Hippo (354–430) said that hymns must consist of three elements – song, poetry and praise of God (to distinguish them from psalms or spiritual songs). He expressed concern that people might be moved more by the performance and the performer than the piece itself and – even more importantly – the message which it conveys. He did concede, however, that the less strong members of the congregation may need to 'take delight in the ears' as a way of 'rous-

very broadly as any kind of poetical composition praising God. Secular hymns also exist praising nature, the state, or some other concept or basic belief, but it is praise of God which characterises the vast majority of hymns written and performed for the last two thousand years, whether or not those singing them were

ing some feeling of devotion'. In some religions, music has been banned altogether; Quakers do not sing in their services; nor did General Baptists for a time. Most churches have always had some musical elements in their worship, however, and the Bible itself clearly refers to hymn singing in many places.

Whereas other, more elaborate forms of religious music have fallen out of favour at times when the churches in which they were performed wished to return to simpler ways of worship, hymns have almost always been found a place because of their communal nature, noted above. As such, they have been especially popular in those eras and denominations which stressed the importance of congregational participation rather than complex musical performance.

An eighteenth century choir (from a drawing by Samuel Hieronymous Grimm. Published by Bowles and Carver c.1770)

Not that the singing of hymns was always welcomed by church congregations. The introduction of hymn singing into Anglican services was never clearly authorised by Parliament, and until the end of the eighteenth century was generally regarded as illegal (though done!). While the practice became more and more respectable as Evangelical clergy introduced hymns with the congregation's approval, as late as 1820 legal proceedings (see page 79) were actually taken against a clergyman for adding hymns to the sung parts of the services in his church! The ecclesiastical court declined to interfere in the matter.

Popularity

The popularity of hymns has also depended on other factors. Reference has already been made to the simplicity of the hymn, both in its music (tune *and* rhythm) and words (verse-repeating). In more recent times, the availability of cheap printing techniques which allowed for the easy publication and dissemination of hymn tunes and texts has increased the popularity of the genre, as has perhaps the ability of people to read words and music. Radio and television broadcasts have also helped to maintain the hymn's popularity.

Some hymns have been popular ever since they were first written and performed. Others have lost their popularity. Writing in 1776, John Hawkins could say of the tune YORK (first published in 1615) that it was 'so well known that within memory half the nurses of England were used to sing it by way of a lullaby; and the chimes of many country churches have played it six or eight times in twenty-four hours from time immemorial'. It is still included in some hymn books and its simple melody would easily be committed to memory, though it hardly rates as an especially popular hymn tune nowadays.

Performance

Much has been written about the way in which hymns should be sung. In the early Middle Ages, many hymns were for performance by a specially trained choir, most church music being restricted to usage in monastic and other great churches, where there were adequate resources for proper and sophisticated music making. The normal way of singing hymns in most western churches has involved a choir leading the singing of the congregation, accompanied by an organ, though for many centuries and in many countries hymns were sung without accompaniment (frequently in unison rather than in harmony) and often outside churches -in the open air, for example!

The tradition of singing hymns in this way dates from the early Christian Church, reappears in the Middle Ages at festival gatherings and pilgrimages and later the eighteenth and nineteenth-century Nonconformist gatherings both in Europe and North America. This tradition has also found its way into secular music-making – not surprising given the close links between sacred and secular as embodied in hymn tunes. Patriotic hymn-singing – notably of Parry's JERUSALEM ('And Did Those Feet, In Ancient Time') at 'The Last Night of the Proms' at the

Wymondham Abbey Choir, 1983

Albert Hall in London, of 'Abide With Me' at Football Cup Final Day at Wembley, or of other 'community' hymns and songs at sporting or national events – is a part of our national heritage.

Because in earlier centuries congregations could not read, it was often the practice to 'line out' the hymn as it was performed. This meant that one of the church leaders – normally the minister or parish clerk – read out each line of every hymn verse before it was sung. It is likely that this practice was adopted when metrical psalms were first used in the Church of England, for example. During the English Commonwealth, the Parliament legislated for 'lining out'. While everyone who could read was given a psalm book and those who could not do so were exhorted to do so, it was recognised that many would not be able to join in the singing, so that 'it is convenient that the minister, or some fit person appointed by him and the other ruling officers, do read the psalm line by line before the singing thereof'.

As can be expected of such a system, the more musical and educated members of the congregation criticised lining out for the way in which it destroyed both the musical and the literary sense of the hymn. The practice remained common until the middle of the nineteenth century, and even then there were protests when it was abolished. It was also common in North America, though there, as in parts of Scotland, the custom was for someone to sing or intone on one note the lines of the hymn before the

congregation joined in. In Scotland, the Precentor, who led the singing, became a powerful figure in the church. A form of intoned lining out, we understand, is still practised in some churches in North America.

Leader

Early English church records also often refer to the appointment of a person or persons who would lead the singing. Reference has already been made to the reading out of hymn texts and the minister or parish clerk would often sing the tune too. This would be especially true in churches where there was no instrumental accompaniment. The leader of the singing was not always necessarily especially musical, and, as Playford said in his 1658 *Introduction To Music*, possessed a 'skill . . . as small as their wages'. The Parish Register of Buxted carries a quaint entry: 'The Old Clerk of this Parish, who had continued in office of Clerke and Sexton for the space of 43 years, whose melody warbled forth as if he had been thumped on the back by a stone, was buried 20th September, 1666'. Not all Parish Clerks were so unmusical. Many of the earliest holders of this office after the English Reformation had started life as professional musicians in the monastic foundations or the larger parish churches which had paid musical foundations. Later clerks often had the sole responsibility for maintaining any kind of musical standard and for choosing the music to be sung, in the absence of any interest or ability on the part of the priest in many cases. William Knapp (1698–1768), of Poole in Dorset, compiled

Instrumentalist from a village choir 'The orchestra was in a short gallery, and presented a most whimsical grouping of heads piled one above another, among which I particularly noticed a pale fellow, with a retreating forehead and chin, who played the *clarionet*, and seemed to have blown his face to a point.' – *The Sketch Book, by Washington Irving. (From The Musical Herald, 1846)*

a collection of metrical psalm and hymn tunes which proved popular in the area near where he lived, for example.

Organ accompaniment
Much singing is accompanied by the organ, though tastes have changed. At some periods of church history, the instrument has been banned. In some denominations, especially in Eastern Europe, hymns – and all other religious music, in fact – are sung unaccompanied, and always have been; instruments – including the organ – are simply not allowed. This was true of the Western Church until the Middle Ages, but the organ seems to have been used by then in the richer churches which could

afford it as a way of leading and accompanying singing and providing musical interludes. The instrument was especially popular in monastic foundations of the Benedictine Order. The organ's loud penetrating tones make it an ideal instrument to lead large congregations, however. Many large continental instruments were designed for this purpose, though they could also be used for sophisticated solo performance.

In Britain, there has long been an ambivalence to the organ as a church instrument. Shepherd, writing in *A Critical Elucidation of the Book of Common Prayer* (1817), said 'The want of an organ cannot be supplied by any other instruments – violins, bassoons, flutes, etc'. However, the Reverend Arthur Bedford published *The Great Abuse of Musick* in 1711 in which he ascribes the poor singing of the time to the bad playing of the organs, where they existed. From the late sixteenth to the late eighteenth centuries, most churches in Britain did not have organs. This allowed a greater emphasis to be placed on the singing than might otherwise have been the case.

William Riley wrote in *Public Music Corrected* in 1762 that organists often spoilt the singing by playing too loudly, by their absurd shakes and flourishes, and by playing interludes between the verses in triple time to a tune in common time! These interludes could last for up to three or four minutes, according to a description written in 1810.

Some of the interludes themselves

were published; they may have shown the virtuosity of the organist,

THE

GREAT ABUSE

OF

MUSICK.

In Two Parts.

CONTAINING
An Account of the Use and Design of Musick among the Antient *Jews, Greeks, Romans,* and others ; with their Concern for, and Care to prevent the Abuse thereof.

AND ALSO
An Account of the *Immorality* and *Profaneness,* which is occasioned by the Corruption of that most Noble Science in the Present Age.

By ARTHUR BEDFORD, M.A.
Chaplain to His Grace Wriothesly *Duke of* Bedford, *and Vicar of* Temple *in the City of* Bristol.

LONDON:
Printed by *J. H.* for John Wyatt at the *Rose* in St. *Paul's* Church yard. 1711.

Cover from The Great Abuse of Musick

but they can have done little for the sense of the hymn or the congregation's involvement in the musical worship of the church. The custom of performing interludes survived into the nineteenth century, including in North America. Occasionally, printed interludes still appeared in nineteenth-century hymn collections, as for example between verses of Charles Vincent's tune SUTHERLAND in the *Hymnal Companion To The Book Of Common Prayer*, where even organ registration directions are included. In the eighteenth century, organists also normally played some composition – or extemporised – three times – as a prelude to the service, before the first lesson or the sermon – and at the end of the service.

Despite these criticisms, good organ playing was extremely popular by the eighteenth century and Anglican churches (the organ was not found in Nonconformist churches until the nineteenth century) all aimed to have a pipe organ when they could afford one. Where the church could not afford a 'finger organ' (i.e. one that an organist played) or where there was not likely to be an organist, barrel organs were often acquired. These had pipes and stops, but were operated by a barrel mechanism instead of fingers and keyboards. The tunes on the barrels were limited in number, though this rarely seems to have caused a problem.

Reforming clergy in the nineteenth century saw the installation of an organ as a way of improving both the standard and variety of church music. Selsey's Psalms (1842), says this of organ playing: 'The organ, it must be allowed, adds much to the effect of Church Music, and by a peculiarly ready construction it is now brought within the range of economy (however limited) of every parish. Its general adoption is strongly recommended and earnestly to be hoped for.' As a way of convincing reluctant congregations that the organ was the best accompaniment for church music in general and hymn singing in particular, many clergy paid for instruments out of their own pockets!

An example of an organ interlude

Church bands

While the organ makes a good accompanimental instrument in large buildings, other forces have been used – such as the church band of bassoon, cello, clarinet, violin and similar instruments, including the aptly named serpent (so called because it was made in the shape of a large snake). Medieval illustrations of music making in the Roman Catholic Church show chime bells, stringed and brass instruments being used in addition to organs. Loud instruments were especially useful for open air services as a way of keeping the congregation together. It would seem that some of the seventeenth century collections of metrical psalms were intended for home use: Allison's Psalter of 1599 includes a lute accompaniment, an instrument

An illustration of a choir in the west gallery.
(Watts, Divine & Moral Songs for Children, 1866)

18

popular in Elizabethan and Jacobean households but not normally one used in church. More recently, brass bands have accompanied open air services, and the guitar has proved popular in many churches as a way of accompanying hymn singing.

The church band in eighteenth-century England would normally be located in the west gallery where the choir (if there was one) would also be housed. At the appropriate points in the service, the congregation turned to 'face the music', so that they could see the leader and hear the band and singers. If there was no band, a barrel organ or a pitch pipe were often used. What instruments were used and the number of different parts of harmony the choir sang would vary depending upon the size of the band and their skill.

There was often great antagonism between the band and the rest of the congregation. The diary of Parson Woodforde of Weston Longville in Norfolk for April, 1793 records that the band and singers went on strike! Only singers and band members were allowed in the gallery – they regarded themselves as an elite.

The life of the village church band is well characterized in Thomas Hardy's novel *Under The Greenwood Tree*. As Hardy suggests, there was much unhappiness when the bands were replaced by an organ and therefore disbanded. In many older churches the band instruments are still preserved.

A good hymn

The hymn – its music and its texts – have been studied extensively by a number of scholars and musicologists. The most famous of these was the Reverend John Julian (1839–1913), whose *Dictionary of Hymnology*, first published in 1892, gives details of over 400,000 hymns (according to the *Oxford Companion to Music*). There are also several societies which exist to promote the study and publication of hymns. Some of these groups are associated with particular religious denominations; some are interdenominational.

What makes a good hymn tune or text? There is no simple answer to this question. The Glossary at the end of the book gives details of a number of well-known, popular or historically interesting hymns and their associated melodies. Not all of these examples would count as great music or poetry, yet many have 'stood the test of time' in that they are still regularly sung in many churches and indeed outside them.

Why should this be so? As far as hymn tunes are concerned, it is likely to be a question of familiarity ('we've always sung this tune – it "goes" to these words') and regular usage (JERUSALEM is always sung at the Last Night of The Proms) combined with simple, singable, memorable melodies which ordinary people find that they can remember without reading or knowing the printed music and which (at least on first hearing) they cannot stop humming to themselves.

Some hymns have special associations for people, either as a symbol of their nationality or the group (whether ethnic, professional or sporting) to which they belong. Most people would also have favourite hymns which have a special message or memory for them as individuals.

Hymn tunes and texts have long been an inspiration for composers. Much German music has been based on the melodies or the words of the great Lutheran chorales. Verses from hymns have been set to music by many composers using different instrumental and vocal forces: Vaughan Williams used George Herbert's poetry in composing his *Five Mystical Songs*; Benjamin Britten, in his church cantatas *Saint Nicholas* (1948) and *Noyes Fludde* (1958) adopted the German Lutheran tradition of interspersing congregational hymns amongst the rest of the music; Carl Orff's *Carmina Burana* uses medieval carols. These are just three small examples of the significant influence which the hymn has had on all kinds of other music.

In the following chapters, we learn of the origin of the hymn, and its development alongside that of the Christian Church, through its various triumphs and failures, its splits and its reconciliations.

CHAPTER TWO

Hymns for the Early Church

I T is clear from even a cursory study of most modern printed collections that the hymn has a long and varied history. One of the very earliest surviving pieces of musical notation – a stone carving found at Delphi, Greece in 1893 – contains two hymns written over two thousand years ago. Music in ancient Greek civilization consisted of five types: Dirges, Songs of Victory, Songs of Revelry, Instrumental music and Hymns – songs in praise of gods or heroes. Each musical form had its own modes, rhythms, harmonies and tunes.

Hymns are also found in the musical traditions of the East. They were sung at special feasts and other occasions, as for example, 'Hymn for the Sacrifice to the Imperial Ancestors' in China. These hymns used modal systems not dissimilar from those used in the early Christian Church, as discussed later in this chapter, and were accompanied by instruments.

The Vedic hymns of ancient India formed an important aspect of worship and, as such, were closely linked to the other parts of religious services, including movement and dance. They were written in praise of the various deities and some date back as far as 4,000 BC. The music was often complex and relied on a sophisticated musical recitation of the texts. Because of this, these hymns were sung not by a congregation but by the priests officiating at the services.

In Mesopotamia and other parts of the Middle East in pre-Christian times hymns and psalms were sung at public services. These pieces were accompanied by instruments and percussion. They may have been sung antiphonally between two groups of singers – a tradition which has long been part of Christian music at various periods.

The psalms of the Old Testament could be classed as hymns in that they are a means of praising God through (antiphonal) recitation. Indeed, some of our best-known hymn texts today are paraphrases of psalms, as for example 'The King of Love my Shepherd is', an interpretation by Sir H. W. Baker of the twenty-third psalm. Other Old Testament texts have been described as hymns, including the Song of Moses (Exodus 15, verses 1–18); the Song of Miriam (Exodus 15, verse 21) and the Song of Hannah (1 Samuel 2, verses 1–10).

It is also clear from other references in the Old Testament that the Hebrews had many religious songs for various occasions and emotions.

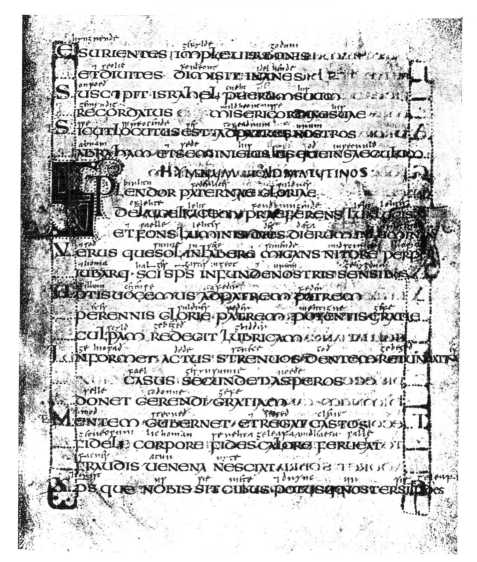

*The earliest English Hymnal (from Historical Companion
to Hymns Ancient & Modern)*

Isaiah 16, verse 10 talks of singing in the vineyards. Psalm and hymn singing was also an important part of worship for other tribes such as the Canaanites and their god Baal. Musical instruments were almost always used to accompany the singing.

The Psalms

The biblical psalms themselves can be divided into those which were primarily for public and those which were largely for use in private devotions. Some of the psalms are songs of praise (Psalms 145, 147, 148), some are concerned with thanksgiving (Psalms 30, 66, 116, 118, 138) and others ask God for assistance (Psalms 44, 74, 79, 80, 83): these three categories could be applied to more recent hymn texts. There are other kinds of psalm in the Bible. The Royal psalms were sung in honour of the King; a number were thought to have been sung in procession at special festivals (24, 48, 87, 95, 100).

What little is known about the performance of the psalms suggests that they were sung only by the Temple priests and not the congregation. As well as instrumental accompaniment, there may have been instrumental interludes between verses of the psalms – a practice similar to that in eighteenth-century England. It is thought that the word 'Selah' between some psalm verses could have been a 'cue' for the performers of these interludes (Psalm 3). The congregation may have joined in the beginning and end of some psalms with the words 'Amen' or 'Hallelujah' (Psalm 104–6, 111–113, 115–117, 125, 146–150). A number of psalms were designed to be sung on pilgrimage (Psalms 84, 122). Psalm 24 was clearly written with antiphonal performance in mind ('Who is the King of Glory? The Lord of Hosts, He is the King of Glory').

The hymn has been part of the Christian tradition from the very beginning. 'After singing the Passover Hymn, they went out to the Mount of Olives' (Matthew 26, verse 30; Mark 14, verse 26). Luke's Gospel includes the Benedictus, the Magnificat and the Nunc Dimittis – all texts which are generally regarded as being hymns and which have certainly inspired many later hymn writers. The Acts of the Apostles and Paul's Epistles also contain many references to the singing of hymns as part of the early Christian Liturgy. The *Odes of Solomon* is a very early anthology of hymns which has survived, albeit not as part of the New Testament. Along with the Psalter of the Coptic Manichean Church, the collection shows how widespread the composition and singing of hymns was in the early Christian Church, especially once it had spread beyond Palestine and shed some of its Jewish ritual.

An important part of early Christian worship, the hymn provided a means of honouring Christ. It also seems to have been used at baptismal ceremonies as a special way of marking the initiation of new members into the community. Hymn texts provided congregations with an opportunity to reaffirm their faith. Most experts on the early church assume that the Old Testament psalms were

A later medieval manuscript (from Historical Companion to Hymns Ancient & Modern)

still sung in the Christian services alongside hymns. The Jewish Psalter was certainly translated into Greek and then Latin. At the end of the psalm was an 'Amen' or short verse such as the Gloria ('Glory be to the Father . . .') – used to Christianise the psalms – which all the congregation could sing.

Hymns also provided the early Christians with a way of reminding themselves of their faith in difficult times. Marcellinus, a late third century Roman Christian buried the martyrs persecuted by the authorities at night and 'cum hymnis' (with hymns). Pope Marcellus, after being released from prison through a miracle, converted the house of his patroness into a church where the two of them prayed together and sang hymns 'night and day'.

Wider influence

The earliest hymns followed the same structure as the Jewish religious songs and psalms, often with congregational interjections and antiphonal singing. As Christianity spread beyond Palestine, church music was influenced by that of other cultures. Greek metrical forms and tonal systems became popular, and two of the very earliest surviving hymns to Christ (one found in the *Paedagogos* of Clement of Alexandria) follow such patterns and modes. The second of these two hymns, the Oxyrhynchis hymn, has partly survived with its music. It is a third century hymn in praise of the Holy Trinity and was written in Greek. It comes from Egypt, where there was a rich church music tradition. Some hymns, such

as the excerpt found in 1 Timothy 3.16, combined eastern structures with Greek styles. The hymn quoted in Paul's letter to the Phillippians 2. 6–11 is very different from Jewish hymns of the period and earlier.

The use of hymns in services became one of the main distinguishing features between the Jewish and Christian liturgies. The early texts and melodies became the basis of the Eastern Roman (and later the Orthodox) Church's hymns, as for example the *Kontakion*. Written in Greek, these hymns were later introduced into France by St Hilary of Poitiers (d c367). It was in the Eastern Church where the hymn became especially prominent as a means of worship, however. As happened in the Calvinist movement of the sixteenth and seventeenth centuries, there was a reaction against hymn writing in the third century amongst the more orthodox factions of the church. It was argued that because hymns were free interpretations of the Bible and not directly based on the Scriptures, they should be banned from church worship.

For a time, this approach prevailed in many parts of the early church. However, the hymn had already proved too popular and the policy had to be relaxed. The temporary ban is nevertheless thought to account for the relatively small number of hymns which have survived from the early church. Hymns were also written by Christian poets for use outside services, as for example the work of Bishop Synesius of Cyrene (c375-c430). His hymn text 'Lord Jesus,

Think On Me' is still found in many hymn books.

As monastic orders developed in the fourth century AD, mainly psalms were sung. In churches open to the public, psalms were sung by a choir trained for the purpose, while hymns were written which all the people attending the service could sing. These hymns were either newly written or were still adaptations of Old Testament scripture or Greek and Roman odes or poems. More recent hymn writers have drawn on existing texts for their inspiration in much the same way. The very earliest western Christian hymns remained primarily paraphrases of biblical texts. The Eastern Church also allowed the performance of religious poems. The Western Church eventually followed suit, initially using the Eastern Church's tunes but later creating its own original melodies.

Traditionally the creator of strophic (verse-repeating) hymns as we know them today was Saint Ambrose (340–397), the Bishop of Milan from 374 until his death. Some of the hymns originally attributed to him are now thought to have been written by others, though this fact does not lessen his contribution to the early development of the hymn. Ambrose helped to develop the basic formula for hymn texts which is still extant. He wrote many hymns in Latin as a way of strengthening his followers in the orthodoxy which he championed and as a way of improving the morale of Christians at times when they were persecuted. Particular hymns were normally associated with different parts of the Church's year (as now) and with the various stages in the daily cycle of services, known as the 'office' and hence the term 'office hymn'. Hymn books such as *The English Hymnal* and its later revision *New English Hymnal* include many of the old office hymns. In the sixth century, the Benedictine Order, founded by St Benedict of Nursia (c480–547) ordained that hymns had to be sung at each of the canonical hours.

Regional variations

The early hymn tunes were based on the chants of the Jewish church, but by the sixth century AD many regional variations had developed. Syria, Byzantium (modern Turkey), Rome, Milan (Ambrosian Use), Spain (Mozarabic Use), France (Gallican Use) all had their own collections of tunes. Despite later attempts to bring these various uses together, notably in the time of the Emperor Charlemagne and Pope Hadrian, many of these different types of chant survived, including that devised by Ambrose, which owed much to the music of the early Syrian Church. St Ambrose's texts still appear in many present-day hymn books, including: 'Come, thou redeemer of the Earth', 'O Trinity of Blessed Light' and 'O Strength and Stay, Upholding All Creation'. One of the very earliest Syrian hymn texts survives in modern hymn books with the words 'Strengthen For Service, Lord, The Hands That Holy Things Have Taken' (usually sung to the tune ACH GOTT UND HERR, a seventeenth-century chorale melody later harmonised by J.S. Bach).

From the fifth to the ninth centuries church music in France was based on the Gallican liturgy. This had its own notation and musical style. St Caesarius, Bishop of Arles from c502 until his death in 542 encouraged the congregation to take part in the singing of church services. He insisted that lay people should learn hymns and psalms so that they could 'sing with a clear and tuneful voice ... so that there be no occasion given in the church for idle talk!'

Because the Gallican liturgy was relatively short lived and universally replaced by the Roman liturgy, little survives, though the hymns composed by Bishop Venantius Fortunatus of Poitiers (530–609) were part of the Gallican tradition. Best-known of these surviving hymns are 'Sing My Tongue, The Glorious Battle, The Royal Banners Forward Go', and 'Hail Thee, Festival Day!' Gallican hymns and other chants were also sung in Ireland. Irish missionaries brought this music to post-Roman Britain, where it was sung until Roman chant was introduced in 597 by St Augustine of Canterbury (d c604).

The Mozarabic liturgy was used in Spain. The term comes from the Arabic *musta'rib*, meaning a Christian living under the Moorish yoke after the invasion of 711, despite the fact that the musical style had largely been codified by that date. The Mozarabic rite incorporates some of the earliest Christian music, dating back as far as the fourth century. Two of the earliest Christian hymn writers Aurelius Prudentius (died c405) and

ACH GOTT UND HERR. (8 7. 8 7.)
Very slow and dignified 𝅝 = 46.

Melody in Neu-Leipziger-Gesangbuch, 1682.
Adapted and harmonised by J. S. BACH.

After Communion.

Liturgy of Malabar.
Tr. C. W. H. and P. D.

STRENGTHEN for service, Lord, the
That holy things have taken; [hands
Let ears that now have heard thy songs
To clamour never waken.

2 Lord, may the tongues which 'Holy'
Keep free from all deceiving; [sang
The eyes which saw thy love be bright,
Thy blessèd hope perceiving.

Seventeenth century chorale, harmonised by J. S. Bach

Caelius Sedulius (died c450) came from Spain. Prudentius is remembered for texts such as 'Bethlehem, Of Noblest Cities' and 'Of The Father's Heart Begotten' and Sedulius for hymns such as 'Why, Impious Herod, Shouldst Thou Fear?'

Almost all the music of the Mozarabic rite has survived to the present day and is still in use in parts of Spain. Mozarabic churches had a different and livelier attitude towards religion than did their Italian counterparts: they often danced during the singing in church!

After the fall of the Western Roman Empire in the early fifth century, Eastern and Western Christian churches developed along different lines, not least in relation to their music. As the Emperor Justinian reinforced Orthodox Christianity as the religion of the Eastern Byzantine Empire, church music flourished. Hymns were introduced in increasing numbers. The subsequent persecution of the eastern monastic orders in the eighth century led not to a decline in musical composition but to a determination to maintain the Byzantine heritage. After the end of the persecution in 842, there was a revival of the hymn writing and composition of earlier centuries.

Byzantine influence
As already noted, the Eastern Church allowed not only hymns based on the Scriptures but also poems with a religious theme. Early Byzantine hymnodists normally wrote both words and music. Many texts were adapted and re-adapted from earlier

sources, resulting in a standard pattern for these hymns. As more and more Saints days were added to the church year, however, there was a need for new hymn texts, though even these were based on the old metrical patterns and often re-used existing tunes.

Until the last days of the Byzantine Empire care was always taken to balance the words and the music of the hymns so that neither element dominated nor was there a loss of meaning in performance. Once the Eastern Empire fell and Constantinople, the capital, was in the hands of the Turks, the great Byzantine hymn tradition almost ceased to exist, not to be revived to any great degree even in the present century, unlike the western Roman Catholic tradition, with its plainsong hymn repertory.

Byzantine hymns used a number of different forms. *Troparia* were verses inserted after certain verses of the psalms as they were sung in church. The *Troparia* developed into compositions in their own right, often linked together in groups, all with the same theme, such as Christ's Nativity. This dramatic element dates back to the early Christian Church; it is also echoed in the medieval mystery play music and the carol.

The *Kontakion* is arguably the greatest of the Byzantine hymn forms. Dating originally from the late fifth or the beginning of the sixth century, the *Kontakion* (the word means literally 'a roll') normally consisted of eighteen or more stanzas all with the same number of syllables and metre.

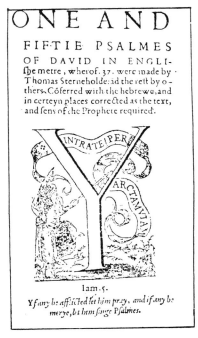

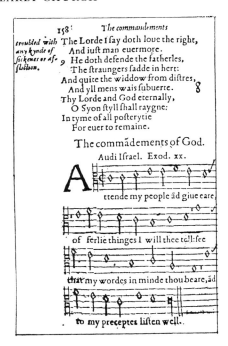

*From the first edition of the psalms printed as a separate section
in the Old Version of the Prayer Book, 1556
(from Historical Companion to Hymns Ancient & Modern)*

Kontakion hymns were written for the major festivals of the church's year.

In the eighth century the *Kontakion* was replaced by the *Kanon*, consisting of nine odes, each composed using a different metre and to a different tune. This was because daily preaching was now obligatory. Since the *Kontakion* had been a form of musical preaching, replacing the sermon, it could not easily be accommodated under the new regime. But hymns were still regarded as a necessary part of the service, hence the *Kanon*, which is still in use today. The greatest writer of *Kanons* was generally regarded as being St Andrew of Crete (c660–c740). Another great hymn writer of the period was St John Damascene (c700–760). A number of his hymn texts are found in modern collections, including 'Come, Ye Faithful, Raise The Strain/Of Triumphant Gladness' and 'The Day Of Resurrection! Earth Tell It Out Abroad', translated into English by J.M. Neale.

The most important centre of hymn composition in the later Byzantine Church was the Studium Monastery in Constantinople. A number of priest-poets continued to write hymns until the tenth century. So prolific were these writers that by the eleventh century the church banned any new composition on the grounds that the existing hymn books were already too full!

The notation used for the hymns of the Byzantine Church differed from that used for the intoned reading of the Scriptures. The hymn notation developed over several centuries, though after the collapse of the Empire, the secrets of the music were largely lost until the manuscripts were deciphered earlier this century. As with Greek and Roman music, Byzantine hymns were written in modes, the forerunners of the modern keys of music.

Other Eastern churches developed different musical styles after the fall of the western Roman Empire. These were the Coptic, Abyssinian and Armenian Churches. The Armenian Church used a notation and a style similar to that of the Byzantine Church; the Coptic Church was based in Egypt and texts were written in Egyptian rather than Greek or Latin. The hymn writers of the Abyssinian Church relied on oral tradition to preserve their texts and tunes, and it was not until the sixteenth century that either music or text was written down. Much remains to be discovered about how this music was performed.

Plainsong

Pope Gregory, who gave his name to Gregorian chant, attempted to codify all the different types of melody or chant in use at the end of the sixth

An example of medieval plainsong with alleluia.

century. In doing so, he aimed at least in part to reconcile the differences between Rome and Constantinople. He is credited with the introduction of a modal system which used eight 'modes' – similar to modern 'keys'- from which the hymn tunes and other kinds of melody were derived and into which they could all be categorised. Eventually, the Gregorian system became the prominent one, and the other Uses such as those listed above fell out of favour or were actually banned by the Church.

As with hymns throughout the ages, the early tunes fitted a note to almost every syllable and phrases were often repeated so that the congregation could more easily remember the melody. A number may have been based on folk melodies which ordinary people would already know – a pattern much followed in later hymnody. Some words – most notably 'Alleluia!' were sung to more elaborate tunes, a practice originating in the Jewish church. Later, medieval theorists created rhythmic modes – standard patterns of note lengths which helped performers remember the music. While the more elaborate plainsong music used free rhythm, hymns and other similar pieces had a definite rhythm which also helped the singers to stay in time with each other, especially when in procession!

Some of the very early Gregorian or 'plainsong' hymns still survive in modern hymn books, though it was only in the eleventh century that the music was written down and the original form of much of the early hymn music is therefore unknown. A typical example of the early Gregorian hymns is 'Audi, benigne Conditor', long ascribed to St Gregory the Great himself. The hymn uses the second of Gregory's modes. Most of the Latin hymn tunes and texts were written by unknown authors and composers, though some are remembered: Paul the Deacon, Rhabanus Maurus, Bernard of Clairvaux and Peter Abelard. Many of their texts are still in use today.

As noted in chapter one, the carol began as a dance song, with a chorus (the burden) and a stanza which varied from verse to verse. The word 'stanza' is almost certain to have derived from the Italian for 'standing' since carols would be so performed. On occasion, carols incorporated parts of Latin text and plainsong into their composition. At first, they were not harmonised, but by the fourteenth century were often sophisticated compositions requiring three or more voices. Unlike many other hymn types, the later medieval carols are often not based on earlier plainsong or folk tunes but are specially composed.

Christmas songs
Carols were normally written in the congregation's native tongue. Because of this, they were a good way of spreading the Christian message, as well as being enjoyable and easy to perform. While many carols were associated with Christmas, other religious subjects were covered in medieval carols, notably the Virgin Mary. Two early examples still survive in many hymn books; they are *Orientis Partibus* and *Angelus ad*

Virginem. Some carols were written with professional choirs in mind and are therefore complex compositions which ordinary people would find difficult to sing; others are simple, folksong-like pieces, most of which would be sung out-of-doors and perhaps in procession as part of some feast or pilgrimage. Some of the carols are linked with the medieval mystery plays, as for example the 'Coventry Carol'.

The later English carol is said to have developed from the French *Noel*. These are Christmas songs dating originally from the fifteenth century. The *Noel* itself derived from the medieval troubadour songs – a form of music which was later to provide the basis of many of the Lutheran chorale tunes. The secular ballad songs also influenced the English carol. The next chapter refers to the effect which the ballad metres had on the later development of hymn tunes and texts. Ballad-carols told a story -usually of the Nativity. There were other types of carol, such as the 'Lullaby' carol, which, as the title implies, were to sing the infant Jesus to sleep. Other carols celebrated the feast of Christmas and the hospitality which people afforded each other at such a time.

Performance

Little is known about the way in which early hymns were performed, though they are unlikely to have been sung in harmony until the later Middle Ages. As already noted, these hymns were usually performed in alternation – one verse would be sung by one individual or group, the next by another individual or group, in the same way that psalms have often been sung.

There are many references in the Old – and some in the New – Testament to musical instruments. These may have been used to accompany the singing or to provide musical interludes between verses in Christian worship also. The latter practice has been used subsequently in both Catholic and Protestant Churches where either the organ or some other group of musical instruments played in between hymns or other choral or congregational pieces.

The later medieval hymn tunes were both popular and memorable. Many of them were adapted by musicians for secular purposes. At the same time, the Church continued to draw on popular music for sources of melodies – melodies which would be well known before they were ever used for liturgical purposes. Indeed, many of the later chorale melodies originated in the Gregorian chants. The chorale melody *Wachet Auf!* is one example of this.

Another is the Christmas carol *In Dulci Jubilo*, whose opening phrase is based on one of the standard Gregorian phrases; so too is the *Kyrie* from the *Missa De Angelis*.

Sacred songs

Sacred texts and secular melodies merged especially in the *Laudi Spirituali* of Italy and the *Cantigas* of Spain – songs which pilgrims would sing as they made their way to the holy shrines or as they took part in penitential processions. These pieces were also used in church plays and many of the *Cantigas* and *Laudi Spirituali* still survive. Some of the latter pieces were written by friars – a brotherhood dedicated to the work of God in the world rather than in the church itself. St Francis of Assisi (thirteenth century) wrote Laudi, some of which are sung today. The most well-known of his compositions is sung to the words 'All Creatures of our God and King'. The text 'Come Down, O Love Divine' also originates from one of the early Laudi.

On special feast days in the medieval church the official liturgy was elaborated with additional music pertaining

WAKE, O wake, for night is flying!
The watchmen from the heights are crying,
Come all ye people to the tryst.

The chorale melody – 'Wachet Auf'

33

to that particular celebration. At the end of some services – particularly Matins, Lauds and Vespers, rhythmic verses were performed instead of the customary concluding plainsong. These verses became known as *Cantiones* or songs and form the basis of many later hymn and chorale tunes as well as the English carol repertory.

Russia was not converted to Christianity until the late tenth century. Much of the work of conversion was undertaken by Greek priests, hence the close links between Greek and Russian churches in later centuries. However, because the Greek missionaries did not understand Russian, monks from Bulgaria were used as interpreters. As a result, the Byzantine hymns and chants which were introduced by the Greeks were sung in a Bulgarian/Slavonic version. The early Russian Orthodox Church added sacred verses, based on the Bible and Byzantine religious legends to this repertory. These early pieces were sung in order to give added emphasis to the message being preached – like the mystery plays of the medieval Roman Catholic Church. The music was simple and memorable – a combination of plainsong and folksong. From the twelfth to the sixteenth centuries, the Russian Orthodox Church developed a large number of beautiful chants.

The earliest Old Slavonic hymn books with music date from the eleventh century. They are closely based on Byzantine originals and use the same notation. Gradually, a local style evolved, not least during periods when, for political reasons, Russia was cut off from more westerly influences. As with much other eastern church music, a good deal remains to be discovered about early Russian church music. Though only a melody ever seems to have been notated, it was customary to harmonise this in performance, even though part-singing has never been formally admitted in the Russian Church.

From the fifth to the fifteenth centuries, the Catholic and Orthodox Churches were all powerful. Between them, they generated a substantial number of hymns during that time, many of which are still sung today – and in many churches not following either the Roman or the Greek creeds. When the well-known collection *Hymns Ancient and Modern* was published in 1861, no fewer than 180 out of a total of 780 hymns were translations of old Latin hymns, often with the original tunes.

In the next chapter, the development of hymns in the Protestant churches which developed in the wake of the Reformation in the fifteenth and sixteenth centuries is described. This led to the development of a different but equally rich repertory of hymn texts and tunes.

CHAPTER THREE

Hymns for the Protestant Church

T HE Reformation of the Church, beginning in Bohemia in the fourteenth and fifteenth centuries, and subsequently in Germany, France and England in the sixteenth century, resulted in the writing – or the re-writing – of substantial numbers of hymns, most of which are still found in modern hymn books and regularly sung in churches throughout the world.

From the ninth century onwards, music in the Roman Catholic Church had grown increasingly elaborate. A second and later a third part was added to the plainchant melodies composed by Gregory, Ambrose and others, and the hymn and psalm music was joined by musical settings of the mass and the daily office. By c1450, much church music was written in four parts and required trained singers to perform it. This meant that the ordinary people could not join in the musical worship of the church but could only participate in the service either by listening or at those points when 'congregational' music was possible.

Simplicity

Bohemia (part of what is now Czechoslovakia) was a Roman Catholic country, converted in the ninth century A D. John Huss (1373–1415) founded the Hussites who, like many of the protestant reformers in the sixteenth century, disliked the more elaborate church music. They advocated straightforward compositions which could be sung and understood by everybody in church. Some even proposed that all music

should be unaccompanied and that instruments such as the organ should be banned from worship. The composition and use of hymns was much encouraged by the Hussites because of this. Simple, popular tunes were adapted to sacred texts written in the language of the people rather than Latin.

DE EVCHARISTIA.

An example from the 'Piae Cantiones'

Both the Bohemian and (later) the Lutheran Churches adapted many of the medieval Cantiones described in chapter two. The best-known collection of these Latin songs (seventy-three in all) was *Piae Cantiones*, published at Greifswald in 1582. Edited by a Lutheran pastor but produced by a Roman Catholic, this collection proved to be the major source of chorale, carol and hymn tunes of the period. Many of the texts from this collection were subsequently translated by J.M. Neale, whose contribution to nineteenth-century hymnody is discussed in chapter four. Arguably the most popular hymn which was originally published in *Piae Cantiones* now in regular church use is DIVINUM MYSTERIUM, sung to the words 'Of the Father's heart begotten'.

Many of the Hussites were later to emigrate to other countries, including Britain and North America, where as the Moravian Church (named after Moravia, the other part of Czechoslovakia where the Hussites first established churches) they continued their practice of congregational worship. John Wesley – whose significant contribution to hymnody is discussed later in this book – became associated with the Moravian Church in Britain. It is from that church that he may well have developed his especial interest in congregational singing.

The oldest Hussite hymn books date from the beginning of the sixteenth century: collections of Czech hymns were published in 1501 and 1505, containing 89 and 400 hymns

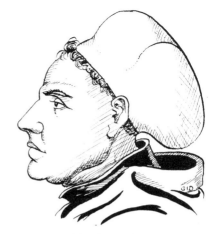

Martin Luther

respectively, while a collection in German, together with music, was published in 1531 by Michael Weiss. These hymn anthologies were much admired by Martin Luther, the great reformer. Later Hussite hymn books brought together large numbers of hymn tunes – many of French origin. A collection published in 1561 under the auspices of Bishop John Blahoslav (died 1571) contained over 750, for example.

German influence
Many well-known hymns originated in the German Protestant Church as founded by Martin Luther (1483–1546) in the early sixteenth century. On 31 October 1517, Luther nailed his 95 indictments regarding the sale of indulgences to the door of the castle church in Wittenberg and started the German Reformation. Luther was himself a keen musician, able to sing and play both flute and lute. It was perhaps his love of music

And good tunes too

Frances Knight on a Victorian polymath

Michael Chandler

THE LIFE AND WORK OF JOHN MASON NEALE 1818-1866

Gracewing £12.99 (0-85244-305-6)

IN THOSE PLACES where traditional Anglican hymns are still sung, the name of John Mason Neale, the Victorian Anglo-Catholic, remains familiar. Thirty-two of his compositions were included in the 1983 edition of *Hymns Ancient and Modern*, more than any other hymn writer (Charles Wesley was next with 29, and then Isaac Watts with 19).

It was, ironically, partly a dislike of the doctrines which he discerned in the hymns of the Congregationalist Watts which caused Neale to take up his pen in the first place. Neale realised that hymns

"A & M" Neale: 32 hymns were his

Grinstead, a community which, in the year

TER
CES

r instance, the
ff, eucharistic and
rship, the role of
ity and decision-
and confirmation.
suggested rules of
the Canons of the
d covering LEPs
ther Churches.

g Unity: A
menical develop-
nties, large cities
f England, is by
athers together the
cumenical inter-
t up by Churches
d (CTE). Work at

intermediate level — between "local" and "national" — keeps local endeavour fuelled, and ensures the exchange of experience and resources, say the Bishop of Liverpool, and the Archbishop of Liverpool, and the Free Church Moderator in their foreword. The handbook covers, among other things, working together on shared concerns like evangelism, local broadcasting, ministerial and lay training, rural ecumenism, and work with young people.

Both books are published by CTE (Inter-Church House, 35-41 Lower Marsh, London SE1 7RL). *Travelling Together* (1-874295-09-3) costs £5.50; *This Growing Unity* (1-874295-08-5) costs £4.95.

Bishop Michael Nazir-Ali has written a book for all those who want to promote the gospel clearly in an increasingly plural world. In **Mission and Dialogue** (SPCK, £8.99; 0-281-04810-X), he says the gospel must be proclaimed freshly in every age; this

attached. So instead they suffer alone.

As one who has been there, I could make a long list of people who have written to me or told me of their experience. Most of them, are women, and many of them are professional people; but the list would also include a managing director, a newspaper editor, a Lord Lieutenant, and many others, including bishops and other clergy, all of them male.

Dr Baker's list would be much longer. He is an experienced consultant clinical psychologist with 15 years' experience of research and of treating this condition. He acknowledges that while working on his manuscript he too was overcome for the first time with an anxiety-and-panic disturbance, and it lasted for eight months. He took his own medicine, and also records how thankful he was that his faith in God held firm throughout those difficult months.

Understanding Panic Attacks is more a handbook than a straight read.

eedom,
ins that
d in-
hem that
evotional
apter,

conveyed it. The second half of the book focuses on dialogue with other faiths, on multifaith worship, and the uniqueness of Christ.

The 65th birthday of Canon Donald Gray is celebrated in the publication of a *Festschrift* on the theme of "the word of God". The book, **Like a Two-edged Sword: The word of God in liturgy and history** (The Canterbury Press, £9.95; 1-85311-115-5), does not mark Canon Gray's retirement: he is Rector of St Margaret's, Westminster, and Chaplain to the Speaker of the House of Commons. But it honours "the significant role he has played in the development of liturgy and liturgical studies in England and abroad", says the book's editor, the Revd Dr Martin Dudley, in his preface. The 12 essays which make up the book are by such well-known scholars as Kenneth W. Stevenson, Michael Perham, Bryan Spinks and Anthony Harvey. **PF**

"understanding is a key word, and a pointer towards "overcoming". Through a deep and sympathetic involvement with the subject, Dr Baker becomes a wounded healer. His brief personal disclosure, in the form of a postscript, will help many closeted people and their families, including some fellow professionals. They will begin to know that they are not alone, and that there is a way to manage this sniping fear.

The layout is busy. A sufferer may not have the concentration to do anything but dip. However, the doctor has demonstrated that he is not afraid to draw near enough to his clients' suffering to be touched by it. He has taken a risk. But it is one which will bring rich rewards.

Grace Sheppard is the author of An Aspect *of* Fear *and* Pits *and* Pedestals.

J

under £15.00

sound Catholic teaching. Indeed, he had few qualms about "improving", existing hymns by changing their doctrinal content, just as he had had few qualms about recommending the improvement of churches through the application of "correct" architectural principles. With Benjamin Webb, Neale had founded the Cambridge Camden Society, whilst they were still undergraduates, to do this,.

As this well balanced biography makes abundantly clear, Neale was much more than simply a hymn writer and ecclesiologist. His achievements in a whole variety of areas were extraordinary. As a scholar he was formidable, steeped in classical and medieval literature, and able to make sense of 20 languages. He was the author of a multi-volumed *History of the Holy Eastern Church*, a work which was to prove crucial in raising the awareness of Eastern Christianity among Victorian Anglicans.

In addition to his hymns and verses, he maintained a prodigious output of sermons, articles, pamphlets and even novels. He was the founder of the Sisterhood of St Margaret at East

warden of some almshouses known as Sackville College, a job which he took because he was fearful of the effects of parochial work upon his indifferent health.

Neale was never far from controversy on account of what others saw as his 'Romanising" tendencies. From 1848 to 1863 he was subject to an inhibition from Bishop Gilbert of Chichester, who believed he was debasing "the minds of these poor people with his spiritual haberdashery". Neale was a ritualist, certainly, but at the moment when he might have departed to Rome, during the controversy over the Gorham Judgment in 1850, he thought instead of the Scottish Episcopal Church.

Michael Chandler's comprehensive treatment of Neale combines a sympathetic understanding of his principles with a critical detachment that does not seek to gloss over some of the less attractive aspects of Neale's personality. It will be important reading for all who are interested in Victorian Anglo-Catholicism.

Dr Frances Knight is a lecturer in Christian theology at the University of Wales, Lampeter.

which encouraged him to found a church where all could join in the singing in order to worship God. Luther wrote that he wished 'after the example of the Prophets and the ancient fathers of the Church, to make German psalms for the people, that is to say, sacred hymns, so that the word of God may dwell among the people by means of song also'.

Unlike many of the later and more puritanical reformers, Luther saw good quality music as an essential part of church worship. He ordered that all his churches should maintain a choir school, and emphasised the value and necessity of music in education. In the preface to Walther's first collection of hymns, published in 1524, he wrote: 'I am not of the opinion that all the arts should be stricken down by the Gospel and disappear, as certain zealots would have it; on the contrary, I would see all the arts, and particularly music, at the service of Him who created them and gave them to us'.

Thus the basic principle underlying the Lutheran chorale – as with other kinds of hymn – was that it could be understood and performed by all the people attending church services and not simply those who were trained in music or the liturgy. The tunes were easy to sing and memorable (many people would know them already in secular versions) and the texts were not in Latin, as in the Roman Catholic Church, but in their own language – German in the case of the chorales, French and English in the case of the metrical psalms which were used in France and Britain in the sixteenth century and later and which developed from the German chorales. The melody was almost always in the tenor voice rather than the soprano or treble voice, as now.

'Chorale' is an English word used to describe the hymns and hymn tunes used in that Church. Germans themselves used the words 'Choral' and 'Choralgesang' to denote any kind of melody used in their reformed church services. The German word Choral is itself derived from the Latin 'Cantus Choralis', referring to the syle of singing plainsong in unison and unaccompanied. Only in the seventeenth century and later did the term Chorale refer to both the text and the tune of Lutheran hymns.

The chorale tunes draw on many different sources. Many of the melodies are arrangements of the older Gregorian plainsong, as in the metrical versions of the *Magnificat* and the *Te Deum*; some are folk songs or other kinds of secular music such as madrigals, re-arranged to suit new, religious texts. An example of this second category is the Christmas chorale *Vom Himmel hoch, da komm' ich her'*, which is actually based on a dance tune/love song with the words *Aus fremden Landen komm' ich her*. Even before the Reformation, there had been a strong tradition in Germany which allowed the use of secular melodies as the basis for church music. Nor had it been unknown in the German Catholic Church to allow the singing of hymns in the vernacular rather than in Latin. *Christ ist erstanden* is an example of an old (twelfth century) German hymn which still survives in modern hymn books – set as an alternative tune for the words 'Jesus lives! thy terrors now' in *The English Hymnal*.

Some chorale tunes – including a number almost certainly by Luther himself (such as *Nun freut euch* and the most famous chorale melody of all *Ein feste Burg ist unser Gott*) – were newly composed, while he also wrote many of the German texts to which they were sung. Initially, several different hymns were sung to the same tune, but as the composition or arrangement of hymn tunes became more widespread in the wake of the development of Lutheranism, most texts had their own tune. In some cases, more than one tune was used to the same text, with different parts of the country using different tunes, as happens in many churches today.

The chorale texts also come from a variety of sources. In the case of Luther's own hymns, for example, some are based on the psalms (*Ein' feste Burg* is a paraphrase of Psalm 46), some are adaptations of Gregorian hymns (*Nun komm' der Heiden Heiland* is based on *Veni Redemptor gentium*, for Advent), antiphons (*Mitten wir im Leben sind* was originally *Media vita in morte sumus*), the Ordinary of the Mass, German sacred song, and non-liturgical Latin hymns. The standard form for the chorale tunes is known as 'bar form'. Each strophe of text consisted of two plus three lines – a grouping similar to the secular songs of the period.

The earliest collection of chorales with which Luther was associated

was the *Achtliederbuch*, which contained only eight hymns (hence its title) and five tunes. Published in 1524 , the book was the work of Jobst Gutknecht, a printer from Nuremberg. The hymns had already been published separately on single sheets the previous year. Also in 1524, two larger collections of Luther's chorales appeared at Erfurt (under the title *Enchiridion*) and Wittenberg (with the title *Geistliche gesangk Buchleyn*). This last book contained music set in up to five parts, arranged by Johann Walther (1496–1570) and with a preface by Luther, which included the following comment:

These songs are set for up to four [sic] voices for no other reason than that I wished that the young (who, apart from this, should and must be trained in music and in other proper arts) might have something to rid them of their love ditties and wanton songs and might, instead of these, learn wholesome things and thus yield willingly to the good.

Another edition of this last collection was published at Wittenberg in 1529. Klug, the publisher of the very first chorale collection, also published a further hymn book that year under Luther's direction. Unfortunately, no copies of this book have survived, even though it was the first collection to contain Luther's great hymn *Ein feste Burg*. Fortunately a second edition appeared in 1533 under the title *Geistliche Lieder, auß neu gebessert*.

In 1545 (the year before Luther

Facsimile of Luther's 'Ein Feste Burg'
(from Hymns Ancient & Modern Historical Edition)

died) the collection *Geistliche Lieder mit einer neuen Vorrede* was published in Leipzig by Valentin Babst. This contained all Luther's hymns, some with tunes by Hans Sachs (1494–1576), one of the last great Mastersingers, immortalised in Wagner's opera of that name – a good example of the close link between the chorale tunes and the popular secular music of the period.

In 1526 Luther published his German Mass. He had already translated the Latin service into the vernacular, but had not been happy with the results – it had not had a German 'feel' to it. Much of his *Deutsche Messe und Ordnung Gottesdients* takes the form of chorales, most of which could be sung by the congregation as well as the choir.

Chorale collections
As the Reformation took hold in Germany and elsewhere, there was a

great demand for chorale tunes and texts. A number of major chorale anthologies were published during the sixteenth century. Walther's 1524 collection had been reprinted in a new edition the following year and was revised and enlarged on a further three occasions in 1537, 1544 and 1551. The first fully congregational book was published under the title *Enchiridion* by Hans Lufft at Wittenberg in 1526. Books were also published at Strasbourg, Breslau and Zwickau in 1525, 1530 and 1537. The following year, the whole Psalter was published in Strasbourg.

Martin Bucer's collection published in Strasbourg in 1541 proved especially popular, not least for its psalm texts and accompanying tunes, many of which were also used by the Calvinist church in their metrical psalter publications. Walther's 1524 hymn book had provided harmonies to the tunes; most of the books printed only the melodies. Kugelmann's *Concentus novi trium vocum* (Augsburg, 1540) arranged a number of chorale tunes for three parts, in the hope that they could be performed nevertheless by 'untrained singers'.

Georg Rhaw hoped to achieve much the same purpose in his school hymn book published at Wittenberg in 1544. Rhaw had been Kantor of St Thomas's Church, Leipzig (where Bach was later to work) until in 1525 he decided to set up his own publishing house at Wittenberg. He drew on his knowledge of the best composers of the day to produce fine hymn books which could be used by both Protestant and Catholic Churches alike. Rhaw (1488–1548) was himself a composer and the anonymous pieces in his various hymn collections are likely to have been written by him.

These chorale collections drew on a wide range of music. Nor were the tunes exclusive to the Protestant Church; settings exist by Roman Catholic composers of chorale melodies, as for example Orlando di Lasso's (1532–1594) setting of *Vater unser im Himmelreich* (The Lord's Prayer). Though not a composer or a user of chorales as such in his music, the great German composer Heinrich Schütz wrote many simple harmonisations of the metrical Psalter. Johann Crüger (1598–1662) was one of the most prolific and effective of the later chorale composers. His tunes include the well-known setting of 'Hail To The Lord's Anointed', HERZLIEBSTER JESU ('Ah, Holy Jesu, How Hast Thou Offended'), RATISBON, SCHMÜCKE DICH ('Deck Thyself, My Soul, With Gladness') and (most famous of all) NUN DANKET ('Now Thank We All Our God'). His chorales were the first to be published with keyboard accompaniment suitable for home as well as church use. A number of famous hymn texts also date from the seventeenth century. Paulus Gerhardt (1607–1676) is especially remembered for his texts 'O Sacred Head, Sore Wounded' (itself a paraphrase of the Latin hymn *Salve Caput Cruentatum*) and 'The Duteous Day Now Closeth'.

Because Luther wanted the congregation to join in the singing of the chorales, it was important to ensure that they were taught the melodies. The more complex arrangements were for the choir only, but the simple chordal settings were clearly intended to be sung by everybody. The Kantor or the whole choir began the chorale by singing the whole tune to the congregation, who then joined in. The tunes were regularly taught in the schools and the school pupils sang in church, as did members of other local organisations who would practice the hymns before the service. While the larger Lutheran churches employed professional musicians to lead the singing, smaller ones relied on these amateur singing groups (*Kantoreien*) or music clubs (*Collegia Musica*) to provide a choir and instrumental accompaniment to the services.

There was a rich and varied tradition of chorale performance in Germany. There was, for example, the technique of *Wechselgesang* or antiphonal singing, which was popular until the eighteenth century and was then revived in the 1920s and became popular amongst Lutherans in North America. This involved the choir alternating verses with the congregation, perhaps even in Latin as opposed to the congregational German. In a sense, this was an elaborate and sophisticated variant of 'lining out', the principle in both cases being that the congregation had to be taught the music and the words before they could sing them.

The chorale melodies provided the basis for a vast repertoire of music for choirs and orchestra, singers and organ. Composers of the German Protestant Church developed the Cantata, a choral composition, often with orchestral accompaniment which used as its basis the text and the music of one of the many chorales known and used by the Church. From 1700, the Cantata became the main form of musical worship in Lutheran churches. A Cantata might include one or more large choruses, solos, duets and recitatives as well as simple settings of the chorale melody, for congregational participation. In each Cantata setting, the appropriate chorale text and its associated melody would be used. J.S. Bach (1685–1750) wrote over two hundred cantatas. One of the best known is that based on the Advent Chorale *Wachet auf! ruft uns die Stimme!* ('Sleepers wake! A voice is calling'). Musical settings of Christ's Passion or Nativity (as for example Bach's *Christmas Oratorio*) also contain chorales for congregational use. The largest collection of chorales published was Johann Balthasar König's *Harmonischer Lieder-Schatz* of 1738, which contained 1,913 tunes.

Initially, the organ was not used to accompany the singing of chorales and what little evidence which survives suggests that Luther did not like the instrument. It may have played interludes between the verses of the chorales. By the latter half of the sixteenth century, however, congregational singing was actually on the wane, with choral performance becoming more popular. Records of the time complain of the lack of enthusiasm amongst the congregation and a number of measures were taken to help lead worshippers, including the placing of trained singers amongst the congregation.

Organ accompaniments

Perhaps because of this, and as a further means of improving the degree of congregational participation in the service, organ accompaniment to the chorale singing became more common. The earliest known printed organ accompaniments to chorale tunes appeared in Hamburg in 1604. Organist-composers such as Samuel Scheidt (1587–1654) provided elaborate accompaniments to the chorales, while eventually, in the hands of J.S. Bach, the harmonisations of the chorale melodies reached a peak of elegance and ingenuity never surpassed.

The chorale, then, proved to be the major inspiration for organ music from the seventeenth century to the present day. The practice of introducing the chorale melody on the organ, and the performance by the organist of interludes between verses and the 'giving out' of the chorale tune on the organ (in much the same way as a modern organist 'plays over' the first line or two of the tune before the congregation begins singing) allowed for the development of the chorale prelude. In the hands of great composers such as Bach and Buxtehude, the chorale prelude became an art-form in itself, capable of showing not only the various colours of the instrument and the technique and sensitivity of the organist, but also of providing a musical meditation on the words of the chorale.

The importance of congregational singing in Lutheran churches varied from area to area. In Northern Germany more elaborate arrangements of the chorales were often sung, and more complex music – such as motets – were also sung by choirs. Some of these compositions had actually been written for the Catholic Church and the books of Rhaw and others show the overlap in musical performance between the two churches. In the south of the country, however, the taste continued to be for simpler congregational music and especially for metrical arrangements of the psalms which could be performed by everybody. These churches were clearly influenced by the strict Protestant churches of Switzerland, where any kind of elaborate music and organs were abolished.

Austere approach

Jean Calvin (1509–1564) was another great protestant reformer who did much to develop the use of hymns in church worship. The Calvinist Church adopted a much more austere approach to music than did either the Hussites or the Lutherans. Instrumental and choral music were banned from their services; instead Calvinists emphasised simple, unaccompanied music. In the preface to the *Genevan Psalter* of 1542, Calvin wrote:

'. . . In truth we know by experience that singing has great force and vigour to move and inflame the hearts of men to invoke and praise God with a more vehement and ardent zeal. Care must always be taken that the song be neither light or frivolous: but that it have weight and majesty, and also, there is a great difference between the music which one makes to entertain men at table and in their houses, and the Psalms which are sung in the Church in the presence of God and His angels'.

Calvin later added that people should not only sing this wholesome and Godly music in church but outside it – in their homes and at work. Given that the emphasis in Calvinist worship was on the Word of God, as recorded in the Bible, hymns written by other than biblical authors were inadmissible. The congregation was only therefore allowed to sing versions of the psalms, usually in the form of paraphrased psalm texts in verse form. This ban on all but psalm-based hymns also extended to Protestant England and – for an even longer period – Scotland.

In 1539, Calvin produced a collection of 'metrical psalms' at Strasbourg. The psalter contained texts and tunes by Calvin himself and the French Huguenot Clément Marot (c1496-c1544). Between 1542 and 1562, a number of editions of Calvin's *Genevan Psalter* were published in Strasbourg, mostly under the auspices of Louis Bourgeois (c1523–1600). These collections aimed to provide simple music which could be performed by a congregation with only limited musical training, though some of the arrangements are more complex, requiring more proficient singers.

John Calvin

The earlier versions of Calvin's Psalter used existing tunes, often printed in Lutheran hymn books. For later editions, Calvin used the French composer Bourgeois to write the tunes. Bourgeois's music was simple, with the melody in the tenor part and the other voices singing note for note against it. Bourgeois later adapted his psalm tunes for use in domestic performances, often with instruments – a practice not to Calvin's liking. The work begun by Marot in writing French metrical versions of the psalms was completed by Theodore de Béze, a Professor at the University of Lausanne.

Like Goudimel (c1505–1572)'s *Psalter*, published in Paris in 1564, Calvin's Psalter aimed to provide a French hymn book which would allow congregations to sing the psalms as part of their Calvinist/ Huguenot services. Goudimel adapted and arranged the work of Bourgeois, as well as composing more complex church music such as masses and motets and secular pieces. He eventually became a Protestant in 1560, being killed for his religious beliefs during the St Bartholomew's Day Massacre.

Like many of Bourgeois's hymns, Goudimel's psalter was primarily intended for domestic rather than church use. The music was simple, although in four parts, with the melody in either the tenor or the soprano part. A Belgian version of Calvin's Psalter appeared at Antwerp in 1555 and Clément Jannequin, though a Catholic, also set these metrical psalms to music in a Parisian publication of 1559.

Many of the texts and tunes from the Calvinist/Huguenot psalters appear in twentieth-century hymn books. Some seventeen tunes written or adapted by Bourgeois appeared in the 1933 edition of *The English Hymnal*, for example. These include the tune RENDEZ A DIEU, sung to the words 'Bread Of The World In Mercy Broken' and a number of those 'Old' psalm tunes which formed such an important part of the later English metrical psalters, discussed below.

Metrical psalter

Gheestelijke Liedekens was the title of a collection of 259 hymns and hymn tunes which was published at Antwerp in 1539. The following year, the same publisher produced *Souterliedekens*, the first complete metrical psalter in any language. Many of the tunes are derived from folksongs rather than being specially composed for the publication. The collection

had appeared in over thirty editions within 75 years of its first publication, including one with 158 settings by the famous Renaissance composer Jacobus Clemens Non Papa (1510-c1568), demonstrating its considerable popularity. It was one of the first sources of the tune THE OLD HUNDREDTH. The *Souterliedekens* collection was intended for domestic rather than church use, though there is evidence to suggest that it was used in the services of the Dutch Protestants who fled to London in the 1540s and 1550s to avoid persecution in their homeland. This was probably the first congregational metrical psalm singing in authorised public worship in England. Clemens Non Papa's edition, published by Susato in 1556–7 consisted of three-part harmonisations of popular tunes adapted to fit the metrical psalm texts.

These psalters proved popular amongst the Huguenot Protestant Church in France until the Massacre of Saint Bartholomew in 1572 and to a lesser extent amongst the more Calvinist churches in Germany. Since both Calvinist and Huguenot Churches eschewed all but the simplest of music, the metrical psalms were sung in unison, though domestic performance of the same pieces could be in harmony.

The psalters were used regularly as a source of texts for Catholic churches. The Council of Trent (1545–1563) had ruled that music should be simplified in the Roman Catholic Church; instruments were not allowed and music based on secular tunes was banned. Like the Calvinists, the Catholics did not favour the use of texts which did not come from the Bible, even in arranged form. These factors must at least in part have accounted for the Catholic Church's interest in the new metrical psalms. As late as 1637, Mersenne was writing that Claude Le Jeune (c1528-c1600)'s metrical psalms should be sung by Catholics because they 'served to incline the mind to the contemplation of things divine'.

Collaboration

Certainly, for much of the period covered by the Reformation in Europe, church music was often interchangeable between Lutheran and Catholic liturgies, and some composers wrote music for both. This allowed for the kind of collaboration which produced the *Piae Cantiones*, referred to elsewhere and for the production of Catholic hymn texts by a Lutheran, with a Protestant commentary (Rhaw's *Liber I Sacrorum Hymnorum*, 1542). Later in the sixteenth century Catholics themselves translated Latin hymns into the vernacular, including the well-known *Veni Creator* and *Veni, Sancte Spiritus*.

The metrical psalters commissioned by Calvin soon proved popular outside Switzerland and France. A number of German translations of the psalters appeared for use in both Calvinist and Catholic Churches. A number of different tunes were composed or adopted for these German versions of the Genevan texts, of which the most memorable musically are those by Jan Sweelinck (1562–1621), the famous Dutch organist.

These are elaborate settings for the most part, however, and were unlikely to have been sung by other than well-trained choirs. The same is true of the psalm settings by Heinrich Schütz.

In France itself the Calvinist psalters remained in use until the end of the seventeenth century, when they were replaced by a number of other psalters which would distinguish the music and the texts from those of the original metrical psalms and psalm-settings, still in use in the Catholic Church!

The Calvinist influence became stronger towards the end of the sixteenth century and there were many demands from within the Lutheran Church for a simplification of the music, which was becoming increasingly complex in some churches, thus excluding the congregation from active participation in the singing. Lukas Osiander (1586) and Sethus Calvisius (1597) also published significant collections of Lutheran hymns. Osiander's *Geistliche Lieder . . . also gesetzt, das ein christliche Gemein durchaus mitsingen kann* embodies the philosophy of congregational participation in its title, as well as being one of the very first hymn collections to have the melody in the treble or soprano rather than the tenor part.

The end of the sixteenth century saw the writing of many new chorale texts, such as Philipp Nicolai's 'How Brightly Shines The Morning Star' and 'Sleepers, Wake!' Also from this period dates the anonymous text 'In Thee Is Joy' (*In Dir ist Freude*) later set to an Italian balletto by Gastoldi and then turned into a famous organ chorale prelude by Bach.

The chorale continued to be significant in the seventeenth century. Eccard (1553–1611) was one of the first to place the melody regularly in the top vocal part and to harmonize it with flowing and regularly moving lower parts, as Bach was later to do so successfully and imaginatively. Hans Leo Hassler (1564–1612) contributed many tunes to the chorale collections of the early seven-

teenth century. He wrote the tune for one of the best-known chorales of all time: *O Haupt voll Blut und Wunden* ('O Sacred Head, Sore Wounded').

Perhaps the peak of Lutheran hymnody was reached with the publication of the collection *Musae Sionae* of Michael Praetorius (1571–1621). This collection, published in nine volumes between 1605 and 1610, contains over 1,200 compositions. Every possible way of setting the hymn and psalm texts is included,

'In dir ist Freude' balletto/chorale

IN DIR IST FREUDE

[OrgelBüchlein – J.S. BACH]

'In dir ist Freude' chorale prelude

46

from the most elaborate chorale settings to the simple three- and four-part chorales which are generally associated with congregational singing. The more elaborate, large-scale works were the model for the chorale cantatas which became popular in the eighteenth century.

The Old Hundredth

Metrical psalms were especially popular in the Nonconformist churches of Scotland, heavily influenced as they were by Calvin. Many of this kind of hymn survive today. The tunes of these metrical psalms – as for example DUNDEE and DUNFERMLINE, from the *Scottish Psalter* of 1615, are simple and easily remembered. So too is one of the best-known hymn tunes of all time, THE OLD HUNDREDTH, so called because it was the original tune sung to the metrical version of psalm 100. Earlier metrical psalm publications which appeared in Scotland were based on the Genevan Psalter of 1561.

1564 saw the first Scottish Psalter (known as *The Old Psalter* or *Knox's Psalter*), printed in Edinburgh. At first only tunes appeared; later editions included harmonisations also. By the mid-seventeenth century, the psalm adaptations of Francis Rouse (1579–1659), Provost of Eton and Speaker of the House of Commons were especially popular in Scotland and many later Scottish hymn books contain his texts. Probably the most well-known text adapted by Rouse was the twenty-third psalm – 'The Lord's my shepherd'.

Given the strong Calvinist tradition in Scotland, it was not until the eighteenth century that hymns based on other than psalm texts were introduced in any great number. The metrical psalm tunes were often elaborated in performance with extra notes.

The publication of hymn books in England lagged behind developments on the Continent. A number of 'primers' were published in the 1530s which included rough translations of latin hymn verses. Coverdale's *Goostly Psalms and Spirituall Songes*, a collection of German hymns and hymn tunes adapted for English use printed in about 1543 was the first English hymn book printed with music. It was nevertheless banned as being too Lutheran, despite King Henry VIII's initial encouragement of the book's production. Copies of the collection were burnt at Paul's Cross in 1546 along with the same editor's 'Great' Bible. However, as the Church of England was formed and Calvinist influences grew stronger, there was a need for simple congregational music, as there had been in Bohemia and Germany earlier. In 1544, Archbishop Cranmer wrote his *Litany with Suffrages* set to 'a devout and solemn note'. This was printed in the 'plainsong' notation which had been in common use since the latter part of the fifteenth century. He also began to translate the old Latin hymn texts into English, encouraging composers to set them to music 'as near as might be, for every syllable a note'.

After the death of Henry VIII in

Title page and a page from Merbecke – 'The booke of Common praier noted'

1547, the Church of England grew closer to its Calvinist counterparts on the continent. All but the simplest church music was banned and only one-note-for-every-syllable settings of words were allowed. Two sets of music part-books survive from this period. Known as the Wanley and the Lumley part-books after their original owners, they contain simple settings of the canticles and communion services, together with short anthems such as Tallis's 'If Ye Love Me' and some metrical psalms.

Book of Common Prayer

In 1549, the *Book of Common Prayer* first appeared. Its principal source was the medieval Use of Sarum, itself based on the old Gallican Rite. The Prayer Book and its later revisions, culminating in that of 1662, which remains in use today, brought together the various monastic services into Morning and Evening Prayer (Mattins and Evensong). The Book Of Psalms was divided into sixty sections assigned to the morning and evening services so that if they were said or sung each day the whole of the psalter would be performed each month.

In 1550, John Marbeck (or Merbecke) (1510–1585) printed his *The booke of Common praier noted*, which later became the basic music for the Church of England's services almost without interruption from that time (though it was rendered obsolete for a time with the introduction of the 1552 Prayer Book). Marbeck used simple, plainsong-like tunes (including earlier plainsong melodies in some cases) to set to music all the main parts of the liturgy. In many churches, both in Elizabethan times and later, the service was largely said rather than sung, despite the existence of Marbeck's simple settings. Music scholars have also cast doubt on whether this music was ever intended for full congregational singing, though choirs of 'volunteers' might have sung it. Though English was now the language of worship, it was still a language which could be understood rather than read by most of the ordinary people.

Psalm collections

Marbeck later produced a metrical text of the *Holie History Of King David* (1579), though this was never set to music. Christopher Tye's *Actes Of The Apostles* (1553) was a series of simple metrical four-part settings of the composer's own version of this part of the Bible. Like many of the metrical psalters, this collection was intended for domestic use, with the music being written 'to synge and also to play upon the Lute, very necessarye for studentes after theyr studye, to fyle theyr wyttes, and also for all Christians that cannot synge, to reade the good and Godle storyes of the lyves of Christ hys Apostles'.

In 1549 two Calvinistic collections of psalms were published. The first was Robert Crowley's *Psalms*, with four-part harmony; the second was a collection of nineteen metrical psalms, without music, collected by Thomas Sternhold, a groom of the robes to Henry VIII and his son Edward VI. Sternhold died later that same year, in which he had also published a further collection of forty-four psalms (still without music), along with John Hopkins (d. 1570) a country clergyman. Crowley's collection was the first complete metrical psalter in English. All the psalms in Crowley's collection were in common or ballad metre; most of those in Sternhold's collection used the same metre.

Despite the completeness of Crowley's book, and the timeliness of its appearance, it was 'Sternhold and Hopkins' as the collection quickly came to be known, that was regularly reprinted, revised and enlarged over the course of the next 150 years. There was a close link between this collection and its continental counterparts, at least in its early editions. During the brief reign of Mary Tudor, England returned to Roman Catholicism and the Reformation ground to a halt. Many Protestants fled to the Continent, taking their experimental hymn and psalm collections with them. Their meetings with Lutherans and Calvinists inevitably influenced their ideas about hymns and hymn singing. Sternhold and Hopkins used the *Genevan Psalter* extensively and in Geneva in 1556, the first edition of their psalter appeared with music. William Whittingham (c1524–1579), later Dean of Durham, was the chief editor.

John Day (1522–1584) produced a music edition in England in 1561 – a timely publication given the ascent

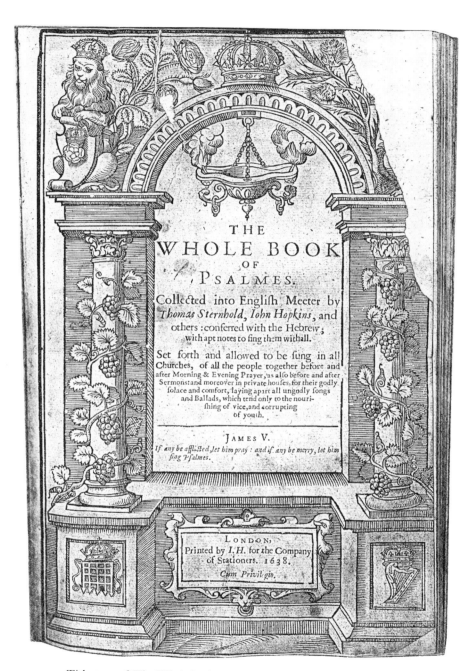

THE
WHOLE BOOK
OF
PSALMES.

Collected into English Meeter by
Thomas Sternhold, Iohn Hopkins, and
others : conferred with the Hebrew ;
with apt notes to sing them withall.

Set forth and allowed to be sung in all
Churches, of all the people together before and
after Morning & Evening Prayer, as also before and after
Sermons: and moreover in private houses, for their godly
solace and comfort, laying apart all ungodly songs
and Ballads, which tend only to the nourishing of vice, and corrupting
of youth.

JAMES V.
*If any be afflicted, let him pray : and if any be merry, let him
sing Psalmes.*

LONDON,
Printed by *I. H.* for the Company
of Stationers. 1638.
Cum Privilegio.

Title page of 'The Whole Book of Psalms' by Sternhold & Hopkins

50

of Queen Elizabeth I to the throne at the end of 1558 and the restoration of the (Protestant) Church of England after the years of Roman Catholicism under Mary. In 1562, Day produced another edition, this time with all 150 psalms included, but only 65 tunes to share between them. Day was also responsible for publishing the metrical psalters of the Dutch religious exiles who came to England because they could not practice their (Protestant) religion at home. Jan Utenhove (1522–1566)'s psalm collection was written for the refugees who founded a community in London in 1544. His psalter *in Nederlandischer sangs-ryme* was first published in 1551. The last edition, printed by Day, appeared in 1566. Other Dutch psalters appeared in Britain, including a 1568 collection for the Dutch Reformed Church in Norwich, Norfolk. This psalter used the texts of Peter Dathen (1531–1588), written in the same metres as the French psalters so that they could use the same tunes.

It is Day's edition of 1562 that most people think of when they refer to 'Sternhold and Hopkins'. The full title page of Sternhold and Hopkins gives details as to when and how the psalms were to be sung:

THE WHOLE BOOK OF PSALMS Collected into English Metre . . .

Set forth and allowed to be sung in all Churches, of all the People together, before and after Morning and Evening Prayer, and also before and after Sermons; and moreover in private Houses, for their godly Solace and Comfort, laying apart all ungodly Songs and Ballads, which tend only to the nourishing of Vice and corrupting of Youth.

Though many of the tunes and texts from the collection remain in use today, their original versions often differ from their modern counterparts. Partly because many of the melodies were based on the old plainsong tunes, the music found in Sternhold and Hopkins used the old Gregorian 'modes' – the forerunners of the modern keys. One example is Tallis's THIRD MODE MELODY, (see p. 52) used by Vaughan Williams as the basis of his *Fantasia on a Theme of Thomas Tallis*. Tallis originally wrote his mode melodies for a metrical psalter produced by Archbishop Matthew Parker (1504–1575) in c1567. Parker had actually written his metrical psalm versions during the reign of Queen Mary for private use.

Use of metre
The rhythms of these early metrical psalms differed too: there were few bar-lines and the number of strong beats varied from line to line. The same was – and is – true of much folk music. One criticism of Sternhold and Hopkins and other British metrical psalters of the period was that too often they arranged the texts according to a metre which was more appropriate to the old-style secular ballad tunes rather than to hymn tunes; meaning and accent suffered in some cases as a result. In fact

THIRD MODE MELODY. (D.C.M.)   T. TALLIS, c. 1515–85
Slow ♩ = 84 (○ = 42).   (*rhythm slightly simplified*).

Third Mode Melody by Thomas Tallis

WHEN, rising from the bed of death,
   O'erwhelmed with guilt and fear,
I see my Maker face to face,
   O how shall I appear?

2 If yet, while pardon may be found,
   And mercy may be sought,
My heart with inward horror shrinks,
   And trembles at the thought;

Sternhold and Hopkins may well have made the metre popular because of their use of it!

While the psalm texts were translated into English and provided with tunes, the old Roman Catholic office hymns (referred to in the previous chapter) and found in the Breviary were not included in the *Book of*

52

Common Prayer seemingly because of the difficulty of translating them effectively into English. In more recent times, thanks to the work of J.M. Neale and others, these hymns have been translated and printed, together with their original tunes and are now regularly sung once again in many churches.

No specific reference was made in the Prayer Book to hymns or to their use at specific seasons – including Christmas – in the ecclesiastical year and such instructions as did exist in Elizabethan England allowed a good deal of flexibility in interpretation. In an Injunction of 1559, for example, Queen Elizabeth ruled that 'in the beginning, or in the end of the Common prayers, either at Morning or Evening, there may be sung an Hymn, or suchlike song to the praise of Almighty God in the best sort of melody and Musick that may conveniently be devised, having respect that the sentence of [the] Hymn may be understood and perceived'. No doubt this was an attempt by the Church of England to satisfy those of its members who would have favoured a more Calvinist approach to worship in general and music in particular, without at the same time encouraging rebellion amongst those still loyal to the Catholic faith.

As the Puritans grew in strength, however, there was less and less tolerance towards other religious views. During the Commonwealth period (1644–1660), for example, Christmas was actually banned as a church festival by Parliament, as it was in the case of the Puritan community of Massachusetts until 1681. Hymns other than those based on metrical versions of the psalms were unlikely to prove popular in view of this. Not until the appearance of the text 'While Shepherds Watched Their Flocks By Night' in the 1700 *Supplement To The New Version Of The Psalms* (Tate and Brady) were Christmas hymns recognised officially.

Congregational singing

The metrical psalters proved so popular because they allowed ordinary people to join in the singing in church in a language which they understood. Moreover, because most churches could no longer afford organs, organists or paid choirs, congregational singing was the only kind of music which was possible. The success of metrical psalmody in this respect is obvious from the numerous editions which were published in Elizabethan and Jacobean England. The year after the full edition of Sternhold and Hopkins was published, Day brought out a four-part harmony version. In line with the performance practice of the period, the four parts were printed in separate part books rather than altogether in one score as in modern hymn books. The 1563 edition by Day had one tune for almost every psalm text, though in fact many tunes were repeated more than once, but in different arrangements.

This set a pattern for later music editions. In 1592, Thomas Este (c1540 –c1608) the great Elizabethan music publisher, issued an edition of all 150 psalms with tunes arranged by the ten best composers of their day, including John Dowland (1562–1626) and Giles Farnaby (c1560–1640). The arrangements range from the very simple to the choral. Unlike most earlier metrical psalters, this one prints the music in score rather than as separate parts. Three of the tunes are named after places – the first examples of this practice, later to become a popular way of naming a hymn tune (see the Glossary for a number of examples). One of the best-known of all hymn tunes first appeared in this collection – and with a place-name – WINCHESTER OLD

Title page of 'The Temple' by George Herbert

– usually sung to the words 'While *Shepherds watched their Flocks by Night*', although a number of earlier tunes were similar to this one.

Many other metrical psalters were produced in Elizabethan and Jacobean England. William Damon (or Daman), a musician at the Court of Elizabeth I, published two books in 1591, one with the melody in the tenor part, the other with the tune in the treble or soprano part. Richard Allison's collection of 1599 shows how popular metrical psalm singing was in the home. Allison composed much music for private use – including madrigals – and his psalter was printed with accompaniments for lute and other domestic instruments as well as with four-part harmony. Edwin Sandys' and Robert Tailour's *Sacred Hymns Consisting Of Fifty Select Psalms Of David* (1615) were also provided with accompaniment for viol, lute or orpharion. John Cosin (1594–1672), later Bishop of Durham, produced *A Collection Of Private Devotions In The Practise Of The Ancient Church. Called The Houres Of Prayer* in 1627. This contains his well-known and much used translation of the Latin hymn *Veni Creator Spiritus*.

Some editors also attempted to extend the range of texts used in these psalters, though with only limited success. William Hunnis (d1597) published *Seven Sobs Of A Sorrowful Soul*, which contained a number of 'penitential' psalms in metre in 1583. Wither (see p. 55) was later to try and do the same. Though never intended for church use, the poems of George Herbert (1593–1632) were later to become popular hymn texts thanks to the Wesley brothers, discussed in the next chapter. His collection of 'sacred poems' was published as *The Temple* in 1633.

1621 saw the appearance of Thomas Ravenscroft (1590–1633)'s *Psalter*. Ravenscroft wrote simple secular pieces such as rounds and catches, published in anthologies like *Deuteromelia*, though it is for his metrical psalm collection (in effect a revision of East's publication) that he is often remembered. Many of the hymns and tunes from this collection survive in modern hymn books, often with the original harmony, including the

placement of the melody in the tenor part, as an alternative to the modern version. An example of this is John Dowland's harmonisation of THE OLD HUNDREDTH ('All People that on Earth do dwell'). Some forty of these four-voice settings are named after places, as for example BRISTOL (usually sung to the words 'Hark the glad sound! the Saviour comes').

George Wither (1588–1667) was a Puritan poet and pamphleteer. In 1623 he published a metrical psalter with the backing of King James I, who wished to see it bound into new editions of *The Book of Common Prayer*. Publishers objected, no doubt fearing for the possible loss of

Loe this is he whose infant Muse begann
To braue the World before yeares stil'd him Man;
Though praise be slight & scornes to make his Rymes,
Begg fauors or opinion of the Tymes,
Yet few by good men haue bine more approu'd
None so vnseene, so generally lou'd.
S.T.I.
Non pictoris opus fuit hoc sed pectoris, Vnde
Diuinco in Tabulam mentis imago fuit.
G.Vl.

HYMNS AND SONGS OF
THE CHURCH

BY GEORGE WITHER.

WITH AN INTRODUCTION BY

EDWARD FARR.

LONDON :
REEVES & TURNER,
5, WELLINGTON STREET, STRAND, W.C.
1895.

Title and facing page of Hymns and Songs of the Church by George Wither

sales of their books! Wither's collection, entitled *Hymns and Songs of the Church*, was notable for its inclusion of the treble and bass parts of sixteen tunes by the great Jacobean composer Orlando Gibbons (1583–1625). These tunes (not all published in Withers' collection) or 'songs' by Gibbons are found in many modern hymn books; they are normally

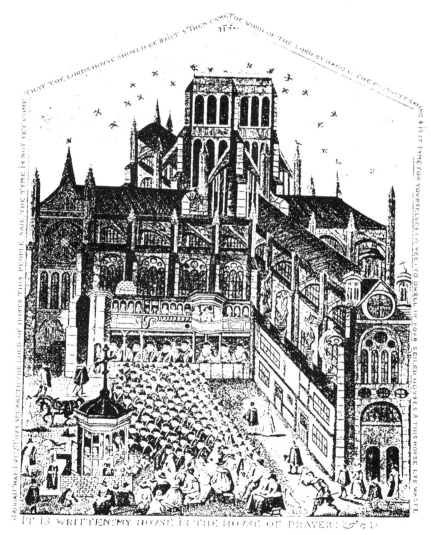

Preaching at St Paul's Cross in the seventeenth century
(Engraving from Wilkinson's 'Londina Illustrata')

named 'song' together with a number (one, two, three). Wither commented ruefully that Sternhold and Hopkins had too much of a hold on English church music but that because of the poor quality of the verse educated people held the metrical psalm in low esteem. Not only that, but because Sternhold and Hopkins's verses could be sung to popular tunes, many of which also had lascivious connotations from their linkage with secular texts, he sought – like the good Puritan that he was – to introduce new and sober tunes appropriate for religious worship rather than singing in the tavern or dancing in the streets. Despite his comments, his collection and Gibbons' music, it was not until Tate and Brady's book and the hymn writing of the Wesleys that Sternhold and Hopkins' supremacy – at least in the matter of the metrical versions of the psalms in general use – was challenged.

George Sandys' (1577–1643) collection of Psalms, published in 1638, contains twenty-four treble and bass parts by Henry Lawes (1596–1662), another well-known Jacobean composer. James I himself is attributed with a psalter, published in Oxford in 1631, though this was actually by William Alexander, Earl of Stirling (d1640) and others and was mainly for use in Scotland.

Psalters were also produced in the Welsh language. William Middleton's *Psalmae y brenhinol brophwyd Dafydh* of 1603 was one of the first. The metrical psalm texts of Edmund Prys (c1541–1624) – also in Welsh – have been used almost continuously since their first appearance in 1621.

Reference has already been made to the publication of the first metrical psalters in Scotland. A further *Scottish Psalter* was published in 1615 by Andro Hart. A second book with that title appeared in 1635. This later publication is generally regarded as the best of the Scottish publications. There were no fewer than twenty-seven different metres, while some of the hymns were 'in reports'. The term 'reports' or 'rapports' was derived from the French 'rapporter' (to carry back) and was a way of describing imitative musical writing. In other words, the different voices imitated each other in their entries, which were set apart from each other like the entries in a fugue or a canon. The music was printed in such as way that a group of singers could stand round the one copy and still be able to see the music easily.

Link with secular music
While the 1635 Psalter was not the first to include more complex hymn settings of this kind, it does codify a practice that was to continue into the eighteenth and nineteenth centuries, when many of the 'Wesleyan' hymns had such imitative writing. These hymns 'in reports' also show a link with secular music of the period, much of which was written in a similar style. What was sung and performed in the home would be easily recognizable and therefore more easily sung in church.

The continued popularity of metrical

psalm singing in the seventeenth century is borne out by the many contemporary accounts of public gatherings at which hymns were sung, as for example at Paul's Cross, London. These occasions must have been similar to the open-air services of the Wesleys in the eighteenth century and the 'revival' meetings of the nineteenth century in America.

Singing texts at home

As already noted, the singing of religious texts was also prevalent in the homes of the gentry and the middle classes. Indeed, it was in private houses that the more complex musical settings were likely to be sung rather than in parish churches for the reason that there were few choirs proficient enough to sing them. During the periods when cathedral music was meant to be simple, metrical psalms were used there too. Canon Peter Smart of Durham wrote that in the early seventeenth century, it was the practice in cathedrals to have early morning prayers 'plainly read by the Minister, with a Psalm in the end, in a vulgar tune, which all the Congregation may sing together'. He also wrote that it was the custom to sing a metrical psalm before and after a sermon, the preacher remaining in the pulpit. It was the custom in many churches for a metrical psalm to be sung while people received communion – a practice still common in some parts of the Anglican Church.

It seems strange that despite the popularity of psalm and hymn singing, there were few attempts to use the melodies as the basis of a school

of English organ composition, in the way that the chorale stimulated the production of so much fine music in Germany. The organ was less important as an accompanimental or a solo instrument in sixteenth and seventeenth-century England than elsewhere. There are settings of metrical psalm texts and tunes by William Byrd and others, though most of these are for voices and, perhaps, instrument, rather than instrument alone.

During the Commonweath period, of course, organs were not allowed in churches and only the simplest of music could be performed – by voices alone – as in Calvinist churches. William Barton (c1603–1678)'s 1644 *Book Of Psalms In Metre* (reprinted 1645) was the official psalter 'printed by Order of Parliament' during this period. Barton does however concede in the preface to his collection that 'the use of an instrument, or observation of a chime, are excellent and speedy means to learn tunes'. Some churches used chime bells for this purpose, while it was often the case that church peals used popular tunes. Instruments would still be used in the home for the performance of psalms. Inventories of the late sixteenth and seventeenth centuries contain many references to psalters, lutes and virginals in the homes of the middle classes.

One example of a tune which was popular as both domestic music and church peal was YORK, usually sung to the words 'Pray that Jerusalem may have/Peace and felicity', a metrical paraphrase of Psalm 122 first published in the *Scottish Psalter* of 1650. The tune itself was published in the *Scottish Psalter* of 1615, with harmony by John Milton (1565–1647), father of the poet. The 1615 *Psalter*, published by Andro Hart, called the tune THE STILT because of its angular melody with its large melodic leaps, suggesting someone walking on stilts. As noted in chapter one, Hawkins' *History of Music* (1776), says that the tune is ' so well known that within memory half the nurses of England were used to sing it by way of a lullaby; and the chimes of many country churches have played it six or eight times in twenty-four hours from time immemorial'.

Rhyming metre

The texts published in books such as those by Barton aimed to return much more closely to the Hebrew originals than had Sternhold and Hopkins, who had been more concerned to put the words into rhyming metre. The same was true of Rouse's work, referred to above. These men were following Calvinist principles which dictated that everything must be based on the Scriptures and those alone. Old habits have died hard in churches from time immemorial, however, and Sternhold and Hopkins remained popular, despite the official support for Barton's replacement.

After the Restoration of the Monarchy in 1660, the old-style metrical psalm was still developed, but alongside it new hymns also began to appear. John Playford (1623–c1687) published a tune book for Sternhold and Hopkins' texts in 1677 which had the melody in the treble or top part rather than the tenor voice (there were only three rather than four parts, as in later books). This was the last complete setting of the old psalm melodies, though it remained popular for the next hundred years, being printed in some twenty editions. Playford's son Henry (1657–c1709) issued a supplement in 1701, including three tunes by the composer Jeremiah Clarke (d.1707).

In 1681, Richard Baxter (1615–1691) produced his *Poetical Fragments: Heart-Imployment With God And It Self*. A number of his texts proved of lasting worth, not least 'Ye Holy Angels Bright'. Baxter was a Presbyterian minister in Kidderminster who wrote the Puritans' answer to the *Book of Common Prayer* which was discussed and rejected at the 1661 Savoy Palace Conference at which a reconciliation between the various Protestant religious parties was attempted. Other hymn texts which have subsequently become popular also date from this period. John Bunyan (1628–1688)'s *The Pilgrim's Progress* produced 'Who Would True Valour See', though this did not become a hymn until the nineteenth century. Bishop Thomas Ken (1637–1711) wrote *A Manual Of Prayers* while teaching at Winchester College. The collection contained hymns, including the famous morning and evening hymns 'Awake, My Soul, And With The Sun' and 'Glory To Thee, My God, This Night' (the latter usually sung to TALLIS'S CANON).

Private publications

A number of hymn books were published privately by churches themselves at the end of the seventeenth century, reflecting the growing interest in hymn singing. In 1688, for example, the parishes of St Martin's-in-the-Fields and St James's, Piccadilly produced such a collection. In 1697, St James's Church brought out its own book. This included a number of popular tunes, including EXETER, otherwise known as LONDON NEW, now usually sung to the text 'God Moves In A Mysterious Way'. These books were the first of many produced by individual churches or their patrons for local use, though a number were to have a wider popularity.

The year 1696 saw the publication of 'Tate and Brady', the eighteenth century equivalent of 'Sternhold and Hopkins'. Nahum Tate (1652–1715), sometime Poet Laureate and friend of the great composer Henry Purcell (1659–1695) (Tate wrote the libretto for *Dido and Aeneas*), collaborated with Nicholas Brady (1659–1726), the poet and cleric, to produce one of the best-known of all the Protestant metrical psalters. Because 'Tate and Brady' was the 'new' psalter, tunes in the 'old' collection (Sternhold and Hopkins) were described as such, as for example THE OLD HUNDREDTH. Tate and Brady's texts aimed to provide more refined words than Sternhold and Hopkins had done.

Until the end of the seventeenth century, Sternhold and Hopkins had been the main hymn book authorised for use in the Church of England, though 'Tate and Brady' soon became as popular. As now, churches preferred one or other collection, depending on their custom and approach to hymn singing. The first editions only contained texts and not music, it being assumed that existing melodies would be used. The 1700 Supplement to Tate and Brady also included hymns as well as alternative versions of the metrical psalms, including 'While Shepherds Watched Their Flocks By Night'. The 1708 *Supplement* to Tate and Brady contained new tunes which have remained popular. These include ST ANNE ('O God, Our Help In Ages Past') and HANOVER ('O Worship The King').

Tune books

Many other tune books appeared subsequently, and in numerous different editions, of which the most popular was *Chetham's* (mis-spelt as Cheetham's in some later editions) *Psalmody*, first published in 1718. This collection introduced a number of new tunes into the hymn repertory. Chetham, who died in 1763, was both schoolmaster and curate in Skipton, Yorkshire. Church musicians of the eighteenth and early nineteenth centuries (especially in the north of England) who wished to make a mark in their profession aimed to have an edition of 'Chetham's' published at some point during their career. A centre of metrical psalm singing which used this particular collection – duly edited and revised by the organists – was Halifax Parish Church in West Yorkshire, where it remained in use well into the nineteenth century. In the 1760s, many of the parishioners had refused to pay for the installation of an organ and taken the Vicar and Churchwardens to court!

Just as Chetham's collection was especially popular in the area near where the compiler lived, so too was William Knapp (1698–1768)'s *A Set Of New Psalms . . . In Four Parts; On Various Occasions*, published in 1738. Knapp was Parish Clerk at Poole in Dorset. The best-known tune in his collection is undoubtedly WARE-HAM. William Tans'ur (1706–1783) was a prolific writer and editor of hymn tunes. He published a number of books, including *A Compleat Melody: Or, The Harmony Of Zion, Containing The Psalms Of David New Tun'd* in 1738. This contains his best-known melody BANGOR, sung to the words 'According To Thy Gracious Word', by James Montgomery (see p. 81).

It must be remembered, however, that few of these collections would be widely circulated; in some cases, they were designed for home rather than church use. As already noted, many of the metrical psalm collections with music used only a small number of different melodies. There would be at least one tune for every different metre; it was unlikely that there would be one tune for every hymn text. Reference is made later in this chapter to the small number of tunes which congregations would know and use.

Chants
Given the popularity of psalms, and the lack of interest in non-biblical texts, it seems strange that it was not until the eighteenth century that the chanting of psalms was practised to any great degree. What are now generally called 'Anglican chants' – short pieces (little more than a few chords in most cases) to which one or at most two verses of a psalm would be recited at a time – first appeared in 1706. A chant published in 1727 and known as Flintoft in G minor was in fact an arrangement of a metrical psalm from Allison's 1599 collection. At least until the nineteenth century, the chanting of the psalms was a practice rarely undertaken outside cathedrals, being therefore regarded as a choral rather than a congregational activity.

The Pilgrim Fathers
Hymn singing soon became popular in the North American colonies which were populated by Protestant groups of various kinds. The Pilgrim Fathers took with them a metrical psalter entitled *The Booke Of Psalms Englished Both In Prose and Metre*. This collection had first been published at Amsterdam by Giles Thorp in 1612 and was used in the congregationalist community set up in Holland by those English people who had fled there to avoid persecution. This collection was edited by the minister of the community there, Henry Ainsworth (1571-c1622). Ainsworth's collection drew on a wide range of English, French and Dutch tunes (thirty-nine in all).

The Bay Psalm Book of Massachusetts was also used in some English churches during the eighteenth and early nineteenth centuries. This had first been published in 1640 under the title *The Whole Booke of Psalmes Faithfully Translated Into English Metre, Whereunto Is Prefixed A Discourse Declaring Not Only The Lawfullnes, But Also The Necessity Of The Heavenly Ordinance Of Singing Scripture Psalmes In The Churches of God.* When last revised in 1773, it had been published in no fewer than seventy editions. Eighteen English editions appeared up until 1754 and the last Scottish edition (the twenty-second) was published in 1759.

The Massachusetts Bay Colony which gave its name to this Psalm Book had at first used both Sternhold and Hopkins and Ainsworth's collection, together, one assumes, with other tunes brought out to the colonies by other religious groups. The first, 1640 edition of *The Bay Psalm Book* was produced because the members of that particular religious community wanted their own collection – the first to be produced in North America. The collection also has the distinction of being printed at the house of the President of Harvard College at Cambridge, Massachusetts. Initially the book contained only metrical psalms, but by 1647 texts not based on the psalms were also being included.

The Bay Psalm Book contained few tunes in its early editions, and as with Sternhold and Hopkins and Tate and Brady, tune books were published to supplement the original compilation. Many of the early American tune books were almost entirely based on British publications. Later American metrical psalters or hymn books often had an educational element, as is evident from the title of the following: *Very Plain and Easy Introduction* (1714), *Introduction to the Art of Singing Psalms, Grounds and Rules of Music* (1721).

Metrical psalms

These various metrical psalters contained the congregational and choral music for churches of all kinds in Britain and elsewhere from the sixteenth to the nineteenth centuries. The metrical psalms provided a way of brightening up what were otherwise remarkably dull services. In the Church of England, the psalms for the day were read out in parish churches, with the minister and the parish clerk taking alternate verses as they sat on the middle and lower levels respectively of the three-decker pulpit so characteristic of the established church from Jacobean times onwards. They would be sung in cathedrals, as they are now, to a special chant, with the two sides of the choir singing alternate verses.

The metrical psalm settings would be more like the modern hymns – a kind of 'musical relaxation' in which all the congregation could join. The more musically elaborate pieces could be sung by a choir (if available), in the way that anthems are sung in churches today. Psalm singing was one of the few parts of church worship in which women could participate equally with men, and as North America began to be colonised and churches built, simple music, as always, was seen as a way of converting and instructing the native population in the Christian Faith.

Over a period of time, and because the congregation learnt both texts and tunes by heart, the tunes – and the speed at which they were sung – gradually altered by custom and practice. It has been suggested that the tempo slowed down during the course of the seventeenth century, partly as a result of the need to divorce serious church music from its secular 'ballad' origins and partly as a consequence of unaccompanied congregations (led only by a parish clerk rather than organ or choir) simply getting slower and slower. The same happens today, both in

'The Chorus' by Hogarth (from the Works of William Hogarth)

63

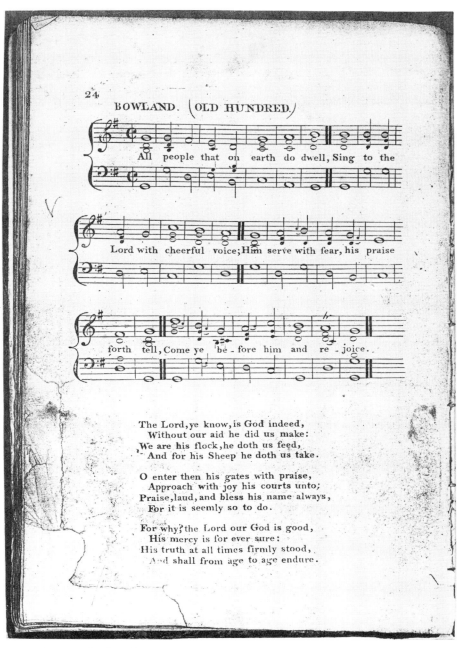

An example of vocal embellishment (from the Musical Companion (2nd edition) to the Psalms used in the Church of St Michael le Belfrey, York)

church and at football matches! Certainly the later evidence of barrel organs (see below) suggests much slower speeds than modern hymn singers would tolerate.

The shape of the melody and the actual notes also changed with usage. As some tunes were altered to fit other texts in different metres, they changed their original time and shape and even their name, in effect becoming a different melody! In some cases, what had been a harmony line or a descant became the melody proper. Congregations still sing what they think is the correct tune and rhythm rather than what is written in the hymn book, much to the consternation of organists and choirmasters!

Not everyone was in favour of metrical psalms or hymns being sung in churches – at least not by a congregation. Dr Charles Burney (1726–1814), the great eighteenth century organist and musicologist, abhorred all congregational singing: he would say that you wouldn't expect untrained people to make shoes – why let untrained people sing!! He did nevertheless contribute some hymn tunes in a collection of 1789.

Burney had good cause for his antipathy towards congregational singing; much of it must have been of a poor standard. Thomas Mace (c1620–1710), writing in his *Musick's Monument* (1676), had said of the psalm-singing of the day: 'It is sad to hear what whining, yelling and screeching there is in many congregations, as if the people were affrighted or distracted'. While Dr Burton, referring to the later psalms with their 'reports' in his journal for 1780 wrote: 'The more shrill-toned they may be, the more valued they are, and in church they sing psalms, by preference, not set to the old and simple tunes, but as if in a tragic chorus, changing about in strophe and anti-strophe, and stanzas with good measure; but yet there is something offensive to my ear when they bellow to excess and bleat out some goatish noise with all their might'.

Another widespread criticism of metrical psalm and hymn singing in the eighteenth century related to the way in which the tunes were embellished by additional notes to the point where the original melodies were unrecognisable. 'Regular singing' or 'singing by the note' became the order of the day as a counter to the over-indulgent 'adornment' of the tunes practised by many singers well into the century.

These additions varied from congregation to congregation and consisted of both trills on particular notes as well as 'slurred' notes added between two or more others. This approach was not dissimilar to the performance practice adopted in other music of the period, where what was written in the music was actually not necessarily what was performed, this being a matter of interpretation for the performers.

Many hymn books and metrical psalters actually give instructions to the singer on how these grace notes and trills should be interpreted. *The Com-*

pleat Psalmodist, published in 1750 by John Arnold (1720–1792) tells hymn singers that 'the first and most principle Grace necessary to be learned is the Trill or Shake; that is, to move or shake your voice distinctly on one syllable the distance of a whole Tone'. Arnold also refers to the 'Grace of Transition, [which is] to slur or break the Note, to sweeten the Roughness of a Leap'.

Embellishments

The effect which these various embellishments must have had on the music, especially when the singers in the choir did them differently, can only be imagined. The congregation must certainly have found it difficult to join in the singing! Old habits died hard, however, and many treatises on good simple hymn singing were published – notably in America – before the practice changed. Why were grace notes and other embellishments introduced? Many of the treatises advocating 'singing by note' comment on the fact that most churches only used some six or eight tunes for the whole of their hymn book or metrical psalter. It is not too difficult to imagine bored choristers (who would be able to read and write) inventing embellishments as a way of keeping their minds on the music as well as showing off their vocal and interpretative talents.

In reading these criticisms of metrical psalm and hymn-singing in the seventeenth and eighteenth centuries, it should be remembered that few people could read or write text, let alone read music. In this context, the many psalm and hymn books of the period did much to support the musical education of the masses, both in Britain and elsewhere. Children were instructed in metrical psalm singing from the 1570s onwards – a tradition which choristers of many generations will testify as providing a good training for later life! Many of the collections already described in this chapter contained instructions on how to sing and read music; some developed an early form of *tonic sol-fa*, a simple way of notating melodies which could be used by even the poorly educated. This tradition of musical instruction through the publication of metrical psalters also developed in North America.

During the eighteenth century in Britain, the teachers of psalmody travelled round the country teaching rural parish congregations how to sing. Psalm-singing was still then extremely popular – too popular for the Bishop of London, who in 1724 wrote to his clergy warning them against 'the inviting or encouraging [of] those idle instructors who of late years have gone about the several counties to teach tunes uncommon and out-of-the-way (which very often are as ridiculous as they are new)'. Singing schools were also popular in North America, and a number of tutors were published, such as John Tufts *Introduction To The Art Of Singing Psalm Tunes* (1721). Some churches were able to form, or re-form a voluntary choir, such as at St Michael-le-Belfrey in York, in the early eighteenth century.

Barrel organs

Despite the problem of embellishments referred to earlier and the increasing ability of some people at least to read music and text, Bishop Gibson preferred the use of 'merely five or six of the plainest and best known tunes', so that everyone could join in the singing. Judging by the barrels on surviving mechanical organs of the period, the advice was generally heeded. Most barrels seem to have fewer than twenty tunes on them. An analysis by Langwill and Boston (referred to in the Bibliography) found no more than thirty different tunes on a total of 63 instruments studied, though only THE OLD HUNDREDTH and TALLIS'S CANON were common to all the barrels. One interesting outcome of a study of barrel organs is the speed at which the hymns must have been sung; a normal revolution of the handle on most barrel organs results in a speed only half customary modern speeds. Little wonder, then, that singers embellished the tune! The same was true in Germany, where the singing of the chorale tunes became slower and slower.

By the end of the eighteenth century, there was a move towards broadening the number of hymn tunes sung in churches and in livening up their performance. More tunes were composed and, indeed, more hymns written. The next chapter discusses the great contribution made to hymn writing and hymn singing by the Wesley family and the Methodist movement. Chapter five looks at the further rise of the hymn in Victorian times.

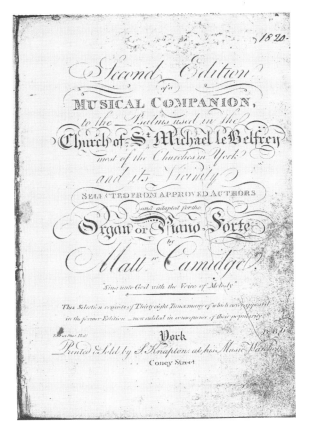

Title page to Musical Companion (2nd edition) to the Psalms used in the Church of St Michael le Belfrey, York

CHAPTER FOUR

Wesleyan and other Eighteenth-century Hymns

F OR most of the sixteenth and seventeenth centuries, the hymns sung in Britain were actually psalms. In some cases, churches actually forebade the use of texts which were not from the Bible; in others it was simply force of habit which precluded the singing of hymns which were not metrical versions of the psalter. This is not to say that such texts were not written before the eighteenth century. George Wither's collection *Hymns and Songs of the Church* referred to in chapter three contained texts which were not metrical arrangements of the psalms, but these do not seem to have been especially popular.

It was not until the beginning of the eighteenth century that hymn books – as opposed to the metrical psalters of Sternhold and Hopkins, Tate and Brady and others – first appeared in great numbers or were widely used in religious worship. In 1707, Isaac Watts (1674–1748), a Nonconformist divine and a prolific writer of hymn texts, published his *Hymns And Spiritual Songs*. This set a new style and standard for the words of hymns which is still the model followed in many hymn books.

In 1715, Watts published his *Divine Songs Attempted In Easy Language, For The Use Of Children*. John Wesley wrote in the Preface to this collection: 'There are two ways of writing or speaking to children: the one is, to let ourselves down to them; the other, to lift them up to us; Dr Watts has wrote in the former way, and has succeeded admirably well, speaking to children as children, and leaving them as he found them'.

In 1719, Watts published his *The Psalms Of David Imitated In The Language Of The New Testament*. In the preface to this collection, Watts wrote that he was not merely translating the psalms, but paraphrasing them so that they could be sung more easily and meaningfully than had been the case with the earlier metrical psalters. Most of the texts in his book were in common, short or long metre; this meant that there were many tunes which could be used in conjunction with them. The title of the book refers to the fact that Watts had said not only that he would 'rejoice to see a good part of the Book of Psalms fitted for the Use of our Churches', but that '[King] David [would be] converted into a Christian'. By this he meant that he was interpreting the psalms in the light of the New Testament. The psalm 'Give The King Thy Judgements, O God', for example, became 'Jesus Shall Reign, Where'er The Sun'.

Watts's texts soon became popular even in the established church (despite the fact that Watts was a 'Dissenter') and most are still found in hymn books. They include 'When I Survey The Wondrous Cross', 'Give Me The Wings Of Faith', 'How Bright These Glorious Spirits Shine', 'Come, Let Us Join Our Cheerful Songs', 'O God, Our Help In Ages Past', and 'There Is A Land Of Pure Delight'. Watts not only attempted to make services more interesting for the congregation, who would only sing a few metrical psalms in an otherwise long and perhaps boring service, but he also offered people an opportunity to sing about the theology of the New as well as the Old Testament.

The increasing interest in hymns, coupled with Watts' success as a hymn writer, encouraged others. Joseph Addison (1672–1719), contributed many hymns to magazines such as *The Spectator* and *The Guardian*. His best-known text is 'The Spacious Firmament On High', first published in *The Spectator* on 23

Portrait of Isaac Watts, after Kneller.

Isaac Watts

DIVINE SONGS

ATTEMPTED IN EASY LANGUAGE
FOR THE USE OF CHILDREN

Facsimile reproductions
of the first edition of 1715
and an illustrated edition of circa 1840,
with an introduction and bibliography by

J. H. P. PAFFORD

London
OXFORD UNIVERSITY PRESS
1971

Portrait of Isaac Watts, after Kneller, and title page of his book of Divine Songs

August 1712. He also wrote 'The Lord My Pasture Shall Prepare', a paraphrase of psalm 23, and 'When All Thy Mercies, O My God', amongst others.

Translations

George I (a German) became King of England in 1714. His accession caused a rise in interest in Lutheran hymns. Johann Jacobi (1670–1750), Royal Chaplain, published a collection of English translations of these hymns in 1722 with the title *Psalmodia Germanica*. Much of the hymn writing of the eighteenth century – including that of the Wesleys, was strongly influenced by that of the German and Moravian churches (John Wesley was for a time a member of the American Moravian Church). James Hutton (1715–1795), a colleague of the Wesleys, later became a member of the Moravian Church in Britain, for which he compiled a collection of hymns 'consisting chiefly of translations from the German hymn-book of the Moravian Brethren'.

In 1737, John Wesley (1703–1791), Church of England clergyman and joint founder with his brother Charles (1707–1788) of the Methodist movement, produced his first hymn book in Charleston, South Carolina. The first London edition was published the following year. This collection drew on a wide range of sources, including metrical psalters, German and Greek hymns in translation, 37 texts by Watts, six poems by George Herbert and a number of hymns by the Wesley brothers themselves. The first

Methodist tune book appeared in 1742. This is the earliest printed source of the tune HERRNHUT, otherwise known as SAVANNAH. The book was known as the Foundery Collection because of the tunes were 'commonly sung at the Foundery, near Upper Moorfields'.

Wesley's hymnbooks

A number of other hymn books were published by the Wesleys' during their lifetime. *The Morning Hymn Book* of 1741 sold for the princely sum of one shilling! This was followed in 1753 by *Hymns And Spiritual Songs*, while Charles Wesley's own 'definitive' (words only) edition of the Methodist Hymn Book (the 'Large Hymn Book') appeared in 1780. This continued to be used for the next hundred years, being almost a 'bible' of Methodism in itself. A revised edition was published in 1831. A musical supplement was produced in 1781. More details about the subsequent publishing history of the collection are given in the next chapter.

The Preface to the 1780 collection makes interesting reading. The publication was regarded as 'highly needful ... for the greater part of the people, being poor, are not able to purchase so many books; and those that have purchased them are, as it were, bewildered in the immense variety. A proper Collection of Hymns for general use, carefully made out of all these books, [was] therefore still wanting; and one comprised in so moderate a compass, as to be neither cumbersome nor expensive'. Because the collection was arranged 'under proper heads, according to the experience of real Christians', it was described as 'a little body of experimental and practical divinity'.

The Wesleyan or Methodist Movement was said to date from 24 May, 1738, and a religious service at which John and Charles Wesley were renewed spiritually, though John had used the word 'Methodist' as early as 1729. The Movement stimulated the writing of hymn tunes and hymn texts, whose performance formed an integral part of their simple yet effective worship, often out of doors.

Portrait of the Revd John Wesley (from an engraving by T. A. Dean)

In their approach to Christianity, the Wesley brothers were spiritual descendants of the Puritans of the sixteenth and seventeenth centuries if not the missionaries of the early church. As in previous centuries, the ability of the hymn to carry basic religious messages, coupled with its musical simplicity meant that it was an ideal vehicle for the Wesleys and other evangelicals after them. The preface to *The Methodist Hymn Book* notes that 'Methodism was born in song'. The two Methodist leaders disliked what they saw as the poor quality verse in collections such as Sternhold and Hopkins and aimed to maintain a high poetical standard in their own hymn texts. In the Preface to the 1780 Methodist hymn collection, for example, John Wesley wrote that in the collection there was 'no doggerel; no botches; nothing put in to patch up the rhyme; no feeble expletives . . . nothing turgid or bombast, on the one hand or low and creeping on the other . . . no cant expressions, no words without meaning . . . We talk common sense, both in prose and verse, and use no word but in a fixed and determinate sense . . .'

Charles Wesley himself wrote the words of over six thousand hymns, many of which are still sung regularly today, appearing in a large number of hymn books throughout the world. The Preface to the *Methodist Hymn Book* notes that Methodism's 'characteristic poet is still Charles Wesley . . . for half a century hymns poured continually from his pen on almost every subject within the compass of Christianity, and while part of the New Testament escaped him, most of all he sang the gospel according to St Paul. He is the poet of the Evangelical faith. In consequence Methodism has always been able to sing its creed'. It was said that Wesley's last words were from a hymn by

Isaac Watts – 'I'll praise my maker while I've breath', published in the first 1737 collection.

Other hymn texts written at this time have proved durable; indeed, some of the best-known and best-loved words date from this period. Among the many Methodist or Evangelical Anglican hymn texts which have become enshrined in popular hymnody are: 'Rock Of Ages' (Toplady), 'How Sweet The Name Of Jesus Sounds In A Believer's Ear' (Newton), 'O God, Our Help In Ages Past' (Watts), 'When I Survey The Wondrous Cross' (Watts), 'Jesu, Lover Of My Soul' (Wesley), 'Hark The Glad Sound, The Saviour Comes' (Doddridge), 'Hark, The Herald Angels Sing' (Wesley).

Many of these hymn texts appeared in hymn collections produced by Wesley's followers (such as Hutton, mentioned earlier). George Whitefield (1714–1770) was a Calvinistic preacher who compiled a hymn collection for his chapel in Moorfields. This was later used at the Countess of Huntingdon's Chapel in Tottenham Court Road. Entitled *A Collection Of Hymns For Social Worship, More Particularly Design'd For The Use Of The Tabernacle Congregation In London* and published in 1753, Whitefield's book is said to have had a major influence on the later Evangelical hymn books produced for the Church of England. This made use of the segregation of men and women in the services by using antiphonal arrangements of texts and tunes, as well as opportunities for women to sing parts of the hymns on

Charles Wesley

their own. Even today, some hymn verses are sung by men or women alone.

Selina Hastings, the Countess of Huntingdon (1707–1791) was herself an interesting character and played a part in the development of the eighteenth-century hymn. The Church of England had an ambivalent attitude to the evangelical ministers whom the Wesleyan Movement encouraged and also to the hymn texts and tunes which they produced for their churches. As noted in chapter one, though hymns were never officially allowed into the worship of the established church, they proved increasingly popular as an alternative to the older metrical psalm texts and tunes which were thought of as dull in the extreme by many as the century progressed.

Conversely, the Anglican hierarchy became less tolerant of the evangelising priests, to the point where they were unable to find parishes. The Countess circumvented this problem by appointing such people to her various chapels throughout the country. In 1779, a Consistory Court decreed that she could no longer do this. She retaliated by declaring her chapels to be 'dissenting places of worship'. In 1780, an anthology of hymns 'collected by her Ladyship' was published for use in these chapels.

Hymn collections

Other Nonconformist church leaders produced hymn books in the wake of the Wesleyan Movement. Philip Doddridge (1702–1751) was an Independent minister working in Northampton who, strongly influenced by Watts' work, wrote many hymn texts. Despite being popular at the time, they were not collected and printed until after his death in 1755. His 'My God, And Is Thy Table Spread' has remained a favourite, not least in the Church of England. It appeared in an Appendix to Tate and Brady published in 1782. One of the early Baptist hymn writers also had the distinction of being the first woman poet to have her work widely used and acclaimed. Anne Steele (1717–1778)'s *Poems On Subjects Chiefly Devotional* was first published in 1760. Like many women writers, she wrote under a pseudonym – Theodosia.

As always when a new movement attempts to sweep away the past, some react against the main trend. One such hymn book editor was William Romaine (1714–1795), who published a lengthy *Essay On Psalmody* in 1775. This included material from Sternhold and Hopkins. Romaine was fighting a losing battle, however. Towards the end of the century a number of collections appeared which became common in the Church of England. These included Augustus Toplady's *Psalms And Hymns For Public And Private Worship*, and John Newton (1725–1807) and William Cowper (1731–1800)'s *Olney Hymns*. This second collection was unusual in that all the hymns were by the two editors and no one else.

Given the fact that so many of our popular hymn texts were written in the eighteenth century, it seems strange that the tunes to which these words are normally sung usually date from Victorian times. It would appear that in eighteenth century Britain the first-rank composers did not write many hymn tunes. As a consequence, in many cases the music of eighteenth century hymn books was of a poor quality. Even the older metrical psalm tunes were badly adapted to the new collections. As in earlier centuries, evangelical priests used secular tunes to help them deliver the Christian message as described in their hymn texts.

Towards the end of the century and the beginning of the nineteenth, for example, some hymn books included a text which was sung to the tune more usually associated with the song 'Rule Britannia', originally composed by Thomas Arne. Arne himself used the tune in one of his anthems, while the words to which the melody was used in hymn books began:

> When Jesus first at heaven's
> command
> Descended from his azure
> throne,

Instead of 'Rule Britannia' in the chorus, the congregation had to sing the words 'Hail, Immanuel'. A few popular choruses from Handel's oratorios still survive as hymn tunes, most notably 'Thine be the glory' from *Judas Maccabeus*. Other, later, collections used the music of the great classical composers of the day

– Haydn, Mozart and Beethoven. William Gardiner's 1812 *Sacred Melodies . . . Adapted To The Best English Poets, And Appropriated To The Use Of The British Church* adopted this approach as a way of introducing lively, well-known tunes into church services.

Many of the Wesleys' own texts were set to music by J.F. Lampe (1703–1751), though few of his tunes now appear in hymn books. A number of his melodies are closely linked to secular music of the time, such as the popular songs from *The Beggar's*

Community singing out-of-doors at Halifax

74

Opera, while others are clearly modelled on the German chorale tunes. Lampe himself was of German origin. On his death, Charles Wesley wrote the hymn 'Tis Done! The Sov'reign Will's Obey'd', sung to the tune REMEMBRANCE in memory of Lampe.

Missions

Despite (or perhaps because of) the poor quality, hymns proved popular amongst the working classes, not least in the north of England where many had migrated to find work in the growing number of textile factories there. These people were ripe for conversion to Methodism and the simple hymns and hymn tunes played a vital role in the missionary work which the Wesley brothers and others carried out during the course of the eighteenth century.

As in previous centuries where 'missionary' work was undertaken many of the Wesleyan or Methodist hymns were sung at open-air religious meetings. These were often attended by several thousand people. At Halifax in West Yorkshire, an industrial town with a long history, records suggest that mass singing took place on Haley Hill on the outskirts of the town in which over thirty thousand people participated.

There are some well-known and well-written tunes which date from this period, including ST ANNE, normally sung to the words 'O God, Our Help In Ages Past', composed by William Croft (1678–1727), organist of Westminster Abbey and the Chapel Royal. Croft also wrote

HANOVER, sung to the words 'O Worship the King'. Edward Miller (c1730–1807), famous as organist of Doncaster Parish Church, is now remembered chiefly for the tune ROCKINGHAM. This is itself an adaptation of an earlier tune TUNBRIDGE, (first published in 1783) now sung to the words 'When I Survey The Wondrous Cross'. Miller published a collection of tunes to be used with Tate and Brady in 1790. Despite his views of hymns and hymn singing, referred to earlier, even Dr Burney, the celebrated musicologist, contributed some tunes to a hymn book in 1781. George Frideric Handel (1685–1759), the great Anglo-German opera and oratorio composer best known for his *Messiah*, also wrote three hymn tunes to texts by Charles Wesley. Probably the best known is GOPSAL, to the words 'Rejoice the Lord is King, your Lord and King adore'.

Inspired by the Wesleys, a number of charitable foundations were established during the course of the century. The most important of these foundations – the Foundling Hospital (with which Handel was closely connected), the Magdalen Hospital and the Lock Hospital – all had their own hymn books. Some of the texts and tunes from these collections are still regularly in use. 'Praise The Lord, Ye Heavens Adore Him' (now usually sung to the tune AUSTRIAN HYMN) comes from a Foundling Hospital hymn book of 1796.

In terms of the development of the hymn, the most important of the

Frontispiece to one of the Magdalen Chapel Books

These pieces developed into what were termed 'fugueing tunes'. The Methodist and Congregational hymn collections still contain some of this kind of music. It is characterised by parts following each other in imitation, as in a fugue, but on a much smaller and simpler scale.

No doubt the fact that the vocal parts imitated each other made it easier for choir members (most of whom would not be able to read music well) to learn a hymn. One of the main criticisms of this kind of music was that it took little account of the sense or the pattern of the verses, and words were often repeated without any logic in order to fit the various melodic lines. This was presumably one of the reasons why eminent musicians such as Burney frowned upon hymns and hymn singing. Some of the better examples of these text-repeating hymns are still regularly used, as for example HELMS-LEY ('Lo, He Comes With Clouds Descending' – one version of which had text by Martin Madan made up from two other hymns!) MILES LANE ('All Hail The Power Of Jesu's Name') and 'O Come, All Ye Faithful', though here the repetition of the text does not destroy the meaning or the metre of the words.

charitable foundations was the Lock Hospital, an institution 'for the restoration of unhappy females'. The principal of the hospital was Martin Madan (1726–1790). He placed great emphasis on musical activity and did much to promote the composition and singing of hymns. As well as the simpler hymns found in most modern hymn books, Madan encouraged the writing and performance of more complex pieces. While still described as hymns, these compositions were more akin to simple choral music or anthems, not dissimilar from the more sophisticated chorale settings in Germany or the music in 'reports' referred to earlier.

Fuges

In America, William Billings (1746–1800), a self-taught musician, wrote many hymn tunes, some with 'returns' or 'fuges'. His 'fugueing tunes' proved exceptionally popular. He also introduced pitch pipes into churches so that the hymns would be sung in a reasonable key. He argued in addition for the use of instruments – such as the bass viol – to accompany their performance. Billings published several collections: *The New-England Psalm Singer* (1770); *The Singing Master's Assistant* (1778); *Music in Miniature* (1779); *The Psalm Singer's Amusement* (1781); *The Suffolk Harmony* (1786); *The Continental Harmony (1794)*.

Few of the hymns in collections such as the Lock Hospital hymn books are now sung, though the tune CAR-LISLE (often sung to the words 'Breathe On Me, Breath Of God') comes originally from this collection. Madan himself was partly responsible for the text of the well-known Christmas hymn *Hark! The Herald Angels Sing*. The 1760 Lock Collection draws heavily on Whitefield's work.

As noted in chapter one, English organists often performed interludes between verses of the metrical psalms or hymns as they were sung. The

*Alternative tune for 'While Shepherds Watched' with fugueing section (from * to end)*

eighteenth and early nineteenth centuries saw the publication of many such collections, similar in principle and approach, though mostly inferior in calibre to their German counterparts, discussed above.

There is little doubt that the hymn as most people know it in the English-speaking world originated in the eighteenth century, with the work of Watts and the Wesleys. That age also saw the gradual decline of the metrical psalm – a decline which became a final demise in the next century – a time when the hymn reached heights and depths like never before. Then the best-known of the eighteenth-century texts were matched with the tunes to which they have been linked ever since. It is from this that the vast majority of our remaining present-day hymn repertory has been created.

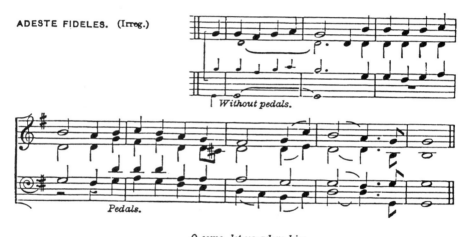

ADESTE FIDELES. (Irreg.)

Without pedals.

Pedals.

O come, let us adore him,
O come, let us adore him,
O come, let us adore him, Christ the Lord.

Repeat section of 'O Come, all ye faithful'

CHAPTER FIVE

Victorian Hymns

B Y the beginning of the nineteenth century, the Church of England
was tacitly allowing hymn singing in its services, though this was
never legalised and in some cases there was fierce opposition to the use
of hymns in churches. Most of the early Anglican hymn collections –
many produced for the use of a particular church or area of the country
– were still mainly composed of metrical psalm texts and tunes rather
than the 'newer' hymns. As noted in the last chapter, there were some
who did not like the changes in musical taste brought about by the
evangelical preachers.

Matters came to a head in 1819, when Thomas Cotterill's *A Selection Of Psalms And Hymns For The Use Of Saint Paul's Church In Sheffield* (first published in 1810) was much enlarged to include no fewer than 367 hymns and only 150 metrical psalms. Objectors took the matter to the York Diocesan Court. The Archbishop ruled that the book would have to be withdrawn and replaced by a revised version, approved (and dedicated to!) him. The resulting 1820 edition had only 146 hymns, though the fact that these were now officially approved was a great stimu-

Diocesan meeting of parish choirs at Salisbury Cathedral
(Illustrated London News, April 1861)

Frontispiece of 'Heber's Hymns', 1867

80

lus to those who wished to introduce a greater variety of congregational music into Anglican services. Even in cathedrals, the singing of hymns (or metrical psalms) became common at the start of the service, and by the middle of the century, 'special services' at which many thousands of people came to sing hymns and listen to the best preachers of the day were widespread. Such services were held in the great buildings of St Paul's Cathedral and Westminster Abbey in London in the 1860s and later.

Thomas Cotterill (1779–1823) later added to his collection with a supplement in 1836; a tune book was published in 1831. Though still for use in his own church, the material was widely used in other parts of the country. James Montgomery (1771–1854) was a Moravian hymn writer who helped Cotterill to compile his hymn collections, eventually publishing his own *The Christian Psalmist* in 1825. His hymn texts were widely used in later books; some remain popular, including, 'Hail To The Lord's Anointed', 'Lord, Teach Us How To Pray Aright', 'Palms Of Glory, Raiment Bright', 'According To Thy Gracious Word', 'Forever With The Lord', 'Songs Of Praise The Angels Sang' and 'Lift Up Your Heads, Ye Gates Of Brass'.

Children's hymns

A number of other collections appeared in the first part of the nineteenth century which were to bring new and lasting hymn texts to a great many congregations in later years. Reginald Heber (1783–1826),

Mrs Alexander

Bishop of Calcutta, had his texts published posthumously in 1827, though many had already been incorporated into other books before then. These included some of the most popular hymn texts of the period and later: 'Brightest And Best Of The Sons Of The Morning', 'Holy, Holy, Holy', 'God That Madest Earth And Heaven' and 'From Greenland's Icy Mountains'. Mrs C. F. Alexander (1818–1895) (née Humphreys) is remembered for her *Hymns For Little Children*, first published in 1848, two years before her marriage to the Bishop of Derry, later to become Primate of All Ireland. The three best known texts from the collection must surely be, 'All Things Bright And Beautiful', 'Once In Royal David's City' and 'There Is A Green Hill Far Away'. The first of these three hymns sums up Victorian attitudes to class: 'The rich man in his castle/The poor man at his gate/God made them, high or lowly/And ordered their estate'. All were to accept their lot in Mrs Alexander's church!

Chancel choirs

The widespread introduction of hymns was part of a much broader attempt to improve the standard of church music composition and performance. It included the abolition of services read by parish clerks from the old-style three-decker pulpits, the abandonment of the practice of 'lining out' discussed in chapter one, the further introduction of organs in churches to the point where the gallery bands became extinct, the use of robed choirs in chancels rather than galleries, and the improvements in education (culminating in the 1870 Education Act) which meant that the vast majority of the members of the congregation would be able to read words and, in many cases, music.

Determined to involve the congregation in the musical parts of the service while maintaining a high standard of repertory, some ministers – notably in the Nonconformist churches – introduced congregational practices. In some places, such as Carr's Lane (Methodist) Church in Birmingham, people paid to learn not only the hymns but the anthem as well! A number of hymn books used largely in the Methodist, Congregation and Baptist Churches actually included simple anthems and chants which all the congregation would be expected to sing. One such example is the *Congregational Church Hymnal* of 1887, which provides a number of simple (and musically indistinct) anthems, including settings of texts from the medieval Advent liturgies which had been revived by the High Church Movement in the Church of England.

Sight singing

The improvements in musical education in Victorian England sprang largely from the sight-singing movement begun by John Hullah (1812–1884) and the Reverend John Curwen (1816–1880). Curwen adopted a system devised by Sarah Ann Glover (1785–1867) of Norwich which became known as *tonic sol-fa*. This system provided an easy means of reading music. It enabled many to join choirs and choral societies who would have found traditional notation difficult to master. The movement was closely linked to the development of education and the improvement of morality amongst the working classes. Writing in 1848, Joseph Mainzer (1801–1851), another leader of the sight-singing classes which became so popular in Victorian times, said: 'Where is the husband debase enough, who would seek pleasure abroad, when the mother sits by the fireside, surrounded by her children, and sings sacred hymns or songs, appropriate in music and poetry, to time and circumstances!'

Congregation participation

The High Church or Anglo-Catholic Revival in the Church of England did much to improve parish church music. The leaders of this revival (including men such as J.M. Neale, referred to below) attempted to return to what they saw as the timeless traditions of Gregorian chant. In doing this, they aimed for the maximum possible participation from the congregation. Chanting the psalms to Gregorian chant, for example, was likely to be more effective in this respect than using what they saw as the less easily intelligible Anglican chant, discussed earlier. By 1843, an Anglican Gregorian psalter, *Laudes diurnae* had been published.

ALFORD.
DOH = Bb.   J. B. DYKES.

:m	f :-.f	d :r	m :d	— :m	s :m	d :r	d :—	—
:s₁	f₁ :-.f₁	f₁ :f₁	m₁ :s₁	— :d	d :d	l₁ :t₁	d :—	—
:d	l₁ :-.l₁	l₁ :la₁	s₁ :m	— :d	m :s	m :f	m :—	—
:d₁	d₁ :-.d₁	d₁ :d₁	d₁ :d	— :l₁	s₁ :s₁	l₁ :s₁	d :—	—

F.t.   f.Bb.

:ᵐl	s :-.s	d¹ :s	t :l	s :f	m :-.d	f :t₁	ᵈs₁:—	—
:ˢd	r :-.t₁	d :d	r :d	m :r	d :-.s₁	t₁ :s₁	ˢr₁:—	—
:ᵐl	t :-.s	s :s	se :l	ta :l	s :-.m	r :f	ᵐt₁:—	—
:ᵈf	f :-.f	m :m	f :f	de :r	s₁ :-.s₁	s₁ :s₁	ᵈs₁:—	—

:s₁	r :-.r	d :r	m :m	— :m	f :r	m :r.d	r :—	—
:s₁	f₁ :-.f₁	m₁ :l₁	l₁ :se₁	— :s₁	f₁ :f₁	m₁ :fe₁	fe₁ :—	s₁
:s₁	t₁ :-.t₁	d :l₁.t₁	d :t₁	— :de	r :t₁	d :d	d :l₁	t₁
:s₁	s₁ :-.s₁	l₁ :f₁	m₁ :m₁	— :l₁	r₁ :s₁	d₁ :l₁	r₁ :—	s₁

:s₁	l₁ :s₁	d :d	r :-.m	f :r	d :-.s₁	m :r	d :—	—
:s₁	l₁ :s₁	d :m₁	l₁ :-.s₁	f₁ :l₁	s₁ :-.s₁	d :t₁	d :—	—
:s₁	l₁ :s₁	d :d	l₁ :-.de	r :l₁	m :-.f	s :f	m :—	—
:s₁	l₁ :s₁	d :l₁.s₁	f₁ :-.m₁	r₁ :f₁	s₁ :-.s₁	s₁ :s₁	{d :—	—
							{d₁ :—	—

' We shall be caught up together with them in the clouds, to meet the Lord in the air.'

mf   TEN thousand times ten thousand,
          In sparkling raiment bright,
        The armies of the ransomed saints
          Throng up the steeps of light ;
f   'T is finished, all is finished,
          Their fight with death and sin ;
        Fling open wide the golden gates,
          And let the victors in.

Hymn tune in Tonic Sol-fa (from The Church Hymnary, 1923)

This was compiled by Frederick Oakeley (1802–1880), the Vicar of All Saints Church, Margaret Street, London, where this type of Anglo-Catholic service was the norm. Oakeley is at least partly remembered for being one of the translators of the text *Adeste Fideles* – 'O Come, All Ye Faithful'.

Improved choir training

Standards of choir-training improved significantly as a result of strenuous efforts on the part of a number of key organist-musicians. In 1841, St Mark's College, Chelsea was formed as a Church of England training college for schoolteachers. The following year, the Reverend Thomas Helmore (1811–1890) was appointed Vice-Principal and Precentor. Choir training and congregational singing to a high standard were part of Helmore's philosophy, as was the use of Gregorian chant.

In 1849, Helmore published a plainsong psalter, which was expanded the following year to become *A Manual Of Plainsong*. As revised by H.B. Briggs and W.H. Frere, the *Manual* has become a classic collection of plainsong canticles, psalms and responses which is still widely used. Helmore also transcribed and edited a number of plainsong hymns, including VENI EMMANUEL, the melody of the Advent hymn 'O Come, O Come, Emmanuel!' In 1852, and again in 1854, Helmore published his *Hymnal Noted*. The following year, in collaboration with J.M. Neale (see below), he published *Carols For Christmastide*; a similar collection of music for Easter was published in 1855.

Helmore's brother Frederick (1820–1899), nicknamed 'the musical missionary', toured the country (in much the same way as the eighteenth-century singing teachers described in the previous chapter) setting up and instructing choirs in even small village churches to sing using his brother's plainsong editions.

Thomas Helmore's work in reviving the old plainsong hymns and psalms was part of a broader attempt to reintroduce music of earlier centuries into church worship. William Henry Havergal (1793–1870)'s *Old Church Psalmody*, published in 1847 was an earlier example of such a hymn collection, though the editor's practice of changing the metre of the originals was severely criticised. The tunes FRANCONIA, sung to the words 'Blest Are The Pure In Heart', and NARENZA ('The Lord Is Risen Indeed') are two of Havergal's better adaptations and are still found in most hymn books. Havergal's son Francis Ridley Havergal (1836–1879) also wrote many hymns, including 'Take My Life, And Let It Be'.

On the Continent, a similar interest was developing in 'early' music in general and plainsong in particular. A number of Cecilian Societies (named after St Cecilia, Patron Saint of Music) were founded. A famous nineteenth-century plainchant hymn collection was published in Mechlin (now known as Malines) in Belgium in 1848. The Mechlin *Gradual* was an attempt to edit medieval plainsong in such a way as to enable congregations to join in during church services. While the editorial process by which this was done is now discredited, the Mechlin style did influence other hymn books and allowed plainsong to re-enter church worship. A number of 'Mechlin version' hymns appeared in *The English Hymnal*, discussed in chapter six.

Cathedral music revitalised

At the same time, British cathedral music – in decline since the first half of the eighteenth century – was revitalised by a new generation of cathedral organists. Men such as Samuel Sebastian Wesley (1810–1876) were both technically gifted and determined to improve the standard of musical performance. As well as composing a number of fine choral anthems and services, Wesley also

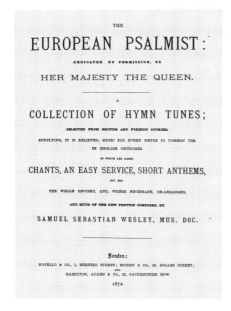

THE

EUROPEAN PSALMIST :

DEDICATED BY PERMISSION, TO

HER MAJESTY THE QUEEN.

A

COLLECTION OF HYMN TUNES;

SELECTED FROM BRITISH AND FOREIGN SOURCES,

SUPPLYING, IT IS BELIEVED, MUSIC FOR EVERY METRE IN COMMON USE
IN ENGLISH CHURCHES,

TO WHICH ARE ADDED

CHANTS, AN EASY SERVICE, SHORT ANTHEMS,

ETC. ETC.

THE WHOLE REVISED, AND, WHERE NECESSARY, RE-ARRANGED,

AND MUCH OF THE NEW PORTION COMPOSED, BY

SAMUEL SEBASTIAN WESLEY, MUS. DOC.

London:

NOVELLO & CO., 1, BERNERS STREET; BOOSEY & CO., 28, HOLLES STREET;
AND
HAMILTON, ADAMS & CO., 32, PATERNOSTER ROW.

1872.

Title page of 'The European Psalmist',
1872

wrote some of the better-known of the nineteenth-century Anglican hymn tunes, such as HAREWOOD ('Christ Is Our Corner-stone), AURELIA ('The Church's One Foundation'), and HEREFORD ('O Thou Who Camest From Above').

In 1872, Wesley published *The European Psalmist*, a collection of psalm and hymn tunes (along with some simple anthems and service settings), including a number of chorale tunes harmonised by J.S. Bach, though these were for practice or home use as much as for singing in church services. The hymn melodies covered all possible metres and drew on a wide range of British and European hymn books, hence the collection's title, though many were written or arranged by Wesley himself. The hymn tune harmonisations were printed with the Alto and Tenor parts above the Soprano and Bass parts, a curious arrangement for the time, but reminiscent of the old metrical psalters and their setting the melody in the tenor part (third part down). Many of the old metrical tunes were included in the collection.

In 1843, Edward John Hopkins (1818–1901) was appointed organist of the Temple Church in London. As with Wesley and Helmore, he set a new standard in church and choral music during his long tenure of office there – a standard which has been maintained to the present day. Like all the organists of the Victorian period, Hopkins wrote many hymn tunes, including ELLERS ('Saviour, Again To Thy Dear Name We Raise') and ST HUGH ('Lord, Teach Us How To Pray Aright').

In 1856, another educational establishment which was to have a profound influence on the music of the Anglican Church was founded. This was the Church and College of St Michael's Tenbury, dedicated 'to the perpetuation of the daily choral service according to the cathedral tradition'. Ouseley was a priest, organist, organ-designer, teacher and composer. As well as choral music, he is still remembered for hymn tunes such as CONTEMPLATION ('When All Thy Mercies, O My God, My Rising Soul Surveys').

Critics

Debates about the kind of music which should be performed in church continued during the nineteenth century. Many condemned the use of elaborate music, as had critics in earlier centuries. One such critic was the Reverend E.H. Bickersteth (1825–1906), editor of various hymnals, including *Church And Village Psalmody* and the popular *Hymnal Companion to The Book Of Common Prayer*. He was a noted Evangelical member of the Church of England and spoke out against what he regarded as musical excesses in church: 'Up to a certain limit, music is the greatest help to devotion; beyond that limit music depresses and dissipates religious fervour'. Bickersteth and others were echoing what St Augustine had said so many centuries before: that music which was too beautiful might detract from the message. 'Better to hear the praise of God heartily sung by the people to a vulgar tune, than an anthem of the highest order performed in the purest style by a dozen

select singers', said Steuart Adolphus Pears in his 1852 pamphlet *Remarks On The Protestant Theory of Church Music*. William Henry Gladstone wrote:

'. . . The spirit of one who writes for the Church must not be that of a mere musician . . . He must be something more. His office has some analogy to that of the preacher. He, too, has to select, expound, and illustrate his text, to dive into its inner meanings, and clothe it in a vesture of song . . . Such was the spirit in which one, whose name has been endeared to

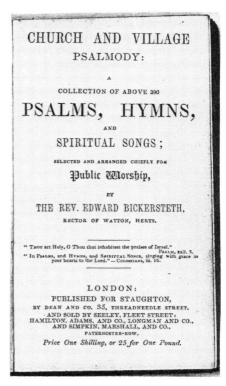

Title page of Bickersteth's Church and Village Psalmody

thousands by his hymns – Dr Dykes – approached his task. Dr Wesley confesses the same'.

New hymn books

All this activity generated a need for new hymn books to replace the old metrical psalter collections, of which Samuel Sebastian Wesley's *The European Psalmist* was perhaps the last example. Vincent Novello (1781– 1861), a Roman Catholic musician, published *The Psalmist* in four parts, the last part appearing in 1843. Novello himself wrote tunes, including the simple but tuneful ALBANO ('Once, Only Once, And Once For All'). Novello's anthology also included organ interludes, discussed in chapters one and three. The same year the *Union Tune Book* appeared.

A revision of Charles Wesley's 'Large Hymn Book' had already appeared in 1831. A further and much more significant revision took place in 1875, when tunes and hymn texts were printed together for the first time. The 'Primitive' Methodists had published their own version in 1825 (revised in 1854), while the 'New Connexion' Methodists also revised Wesley's original 1780 compilation in 1834: all very confusing! A chorister at Magdalen College, Oxford, Richard Redhead (1820–1901) published *Church Hymn Tunes For The Several Seasons Of The Year* in 1853; this contained the tune PETRA, now linked with Toplady's 'Rock Of Ages'. Bickersteth, the critic of elaborate church music and later Bishop of Exeter, writing in 1847, said that his *Christian Psalmody* had 'been so acceptable to the

Churches in our land' that over 128,000 copies had been sold. A selected edition, *Church and Village Psalmody* was published that year for congregations chiefly of the poor, hence the selection – sold at half-the-price of the full volume! Bickersteth's collection is one of a number where hymns are printed alongside the old metrical psalms, so catering for all tastes.

Many of the earlier collections had separated the tune book from the hymn book and only a small group of singers or the band leader would have music; everybody else would use words-only copies, as happens in most churches today. Tunes were composed especially for these new nineteenth-century collections, such as BELGRAVE ('When All Thy Mercies, O My God') and HORSLEY ('There Is A Green Hill Far Away') written by William Horsley (1774– 1858) and WESTMINSTER ('My God, How Wonderful Thou Art') written by James Turle (1802– 1882), sometime organist of the Abbey after which the tune is named. Some tune books were designed to service several different collections of texts, as for example Henry Allon and Henry John Gauntlett's *The Congregational Psalmist: A Companion To The New Congregational, The New Baptist, And The Leeds Hymn-Books* . . . (1858).

Hymns A & M

1861 was a landmark, for in that year, *Hymns Ancient and Modern* was published. Though by this time several hymn books had been published, and Tate and Brady, the dominant metrical psalter of the nineteenth century, was waning in popularity, it was this particular collection which came to symbolise hymn singing and hymn books for many people. Initially a collection produced by the Tractarian Movement, *Hymns Ancient and Modern* became widely accepted, and was the standard hymn book in many Anglican churches throughout the country and also abroad. Well over 150 million copies were sold in the first hundred years of the book's existence. For many, 'Hymns A & M' as it was often known, was *the* hymn book. Many choristers were brought up using it and organists of countless generations knew the hymn numbers by heart.

A trial edition of *Hymns A & M* had been released in 1860, and the first full edition of 1861 contained 273 hymns. An Appendix appeared in 1868 which brought the total to 386. A revised edition was published in 1875 and contained 473 hymns, to which was added a further supplement in 1889, bringing the total number of hymns to 638. A new edition was produced in 1904 with 643 hymns, though this did not replace the old edition in popularity. It was said that one of the difficulties with this book was that the hymn numbers of tunes and texts in the earlier editions had changed and people objected because many knew the original numbers off by heart! The original edition, together with a second supplement published in 1916 remained in regular use as a result. The Standard Edition (in effect the 1875 edition together with

the second supplement) appeared in 1922, with 779 hymns. This was eventually replaced by *Hymns Ancient and Modern Revised* in 1950. A supplement to this edition, *100 Hymns For Today* was published in 1969, a second supplement (*More Hymns For Today*) appearing in 1980. These two supplements, and an abridgement of 333 hymns from *Hymns A & M Revised*, were published together as the *New Standard Hymns Ancient and Modern* in 1983. In ten years, sales of one million copies have been recorded. A full history of the first 100 years of *Hymns Ancient and Modern* has been published and is listed in the bibliography at the end of this book.

The 1861 hymn book set a style and a standard that was not to be changed significantly until the appearance of *The English Hymnal*, discussed in the next chapter. Intended as a complement to the Prayer Book, the collection was arranged in much the same order. It was one of the first hymn books to have a tune printed for every text – usually one to a page – and to adopt a policy of printing 'Amen' at the end of every one. More importantly, it was in *Hymns Ancient and Modern* that many tunes and texts were brought together in durable pairings which are still favoured. While today hymn singers assume that certain hymn texts have always been sung to a particular tune, in many cases this was not so until they appeared together in the 1861 collection.

Hymn books such as *Hymns Ancient and Modern* drew on a wide range of

The Revd J. M. Neale

was both Chairman of the Proprietors of the publication and a writer and translator of many well-known hymn texts, including 'Lord, Thy Word Abideth', and 'The King Of Love My Shepherd Is'; W.H. Monk (1823–1889) Organist of King's College, London, The Reverend J.B. Dykes (1823–1876), Precentor of Durham Cathedral and Sir John Stainer (1840–1901), Organist of St Paul's Cathedral, London. Monk and Stainer edited and contributed to many hymn books during the course of their careers, not least *Hymns Ancient and Modern*.

Dykes is remembered as the Victorian hymn tune composer *par excellence*. Many of the best-known hymn tunes were written by him. They include DOMINUS REGIT ME ('The King Of Love My Shepherd Is'), GERONTIUS ('Praise To The Holiest In The Height'), MELITA ('Eternal Father, Strong To Save'), NICAEA ('Holy, Holy, Holy, Lord God Almighty'), and ST CUTHBERT ('Our Blest Redeemer, Ere He Breathed'). Not all are as well-composed or as memorable as these examples, however, and many of his 276 hymn tunes (published collectively in 1901) are now largely forgotten.

musical and literary sources. One of the most prolific writers and translators was the Reverend John Mason Neale (1818–1866), an Anglo-Catholic divine. Neale was closely associated with the Ecclesiological Society, which aimed to inculcate Catholic traditions in all aspects of the Anglican Church. As a result, Neale translated many of the early Latin hymns into English, such as *Pange Lingua*, *Veni Sancte Spiritus* and *O Salutaris Hostia*. Approximately one-eighth of the texts in the 1861 edition of *Hymns Ancient and Modern* are written or translated by him. In 1865, Neale published his *Hymns Chiefly Medieval, Of The Joys And Glories Of Paradise*.

Four men were closely associated with the music of *Hymns Ancient and Modern*. They were: Sir H.W. Baker (1821–1877), a Baronet and Vicar of Monkland in Herefordshire, who

Monk wrote EVENTIDE ('Abide With Me, Fast Falls The Eventide'), one of the most frequently sung hymn tunes of all time. Stainer, now best remembered for his Passiontide cantata for chorus, soloists and organ, also contributed a number of hymn tunes (including LOVE DIVINE, often performed to the

The Revd J. B. Dykes

words 'Love Divine, All Loves Excelling', frequently used in Anglican wedding services and CHARITY – 'Gracious Spirit, Holy Ghost') to the many hymn books with which he was associated. *The Crucifixion* contains arguably his best-remembered hymn tunes, such as CROSS OF JESUS.

Like Samuel Sebastian Wesley before him, Stainer did much to improve the standard of cathedral music during his time as Organist of St Paul's Cathedral (1872–1898) as well as to increase interest in early music, including plainsong. He supervised the revision of Helmore's *A Manual of Plainsong* by Briggs and Frere. He wrote a total of 158 hymn tunes which were published together in 1900.

More prolific even than J. B. Dykes as a hymn tune writer was H.J. Gauntlett (1805–1876), a largely self-taught musician who eventually graduated D.Mus., claimed to have written over ten thousand hymn tunes, and while many are still regularly sung, it would be difficult to trace so many! Gauntlett's best-known tune must be IRBY, now invariably sung to the words 'Once In Royal David's City'. Also popular is his ST ALBINUS, sung to the words 'Jesus Lives! Thy Terrors Now'. Gauntlett was also an expert in pipe organ design, and had a considerable influence on the development of the instrument in the nineteenth century. He was keen to increase the power of the instrument so that it could lead the singing of large congregations. Many of the early instruments which he planned were in Nonconformist churches which, when they eventually allowed instruments in their buildings, would require loud and penetrating sounds which would be heard above hundreds of voices.

Sir Arthur Sullivan (1842–1900) is primarily remembered for his operettas, written in conjunction with Sir W.S. Gilbert. However, for much of his life, Sullivan had a connection with the church and his is an important contribution to hymnody, writing some fifty-six hymn tunes during the course of his life. These were published under a single cover in 1902. His early training was as a chorister at the Chapel Royal, where he came under the influence of Thomas Helmore, by then Master of the Choristers there. Recognizing Sullivan's talent, Helmore encouraged the boy to compose hymn and psalm tunes, as well as other, grander works.

In 1861, Sullivan became organist of St Michael's Chester Square, a fashionable London church, moving to a more prestigious appointment at St Peter's, Cranley Gardens in 1867. He was responsible for some of the most memorable of the Victorian hymn tunes, such as LUX EOI ('Alleluia! Alleluia! Hearts To Heaven And Voices Raise'), GOLDEN SHEAVES ('To Thee, O Lord, Our Hearts We Raise') and ST GERTRUDE ('Onward Christian Soldiers!') as well as the first dynamic markings in hymn books. Sullivan edited the 1874 edition of *Church Hymns*, published by the Society For The Promotion Of Christian Knowledge and one of the few rivals to *Hymns Ancient and Modern* at the time.

There were many other musicians and composers whose hymn tunes appeared in the various editions of *Hymns Ancient and Modern*. Some were well-known in their day, others were amateurs who wrote one or two tunes which caught the imagination of the hymn book compilers and proved to be popular amongst congregations. Captain A. Ewing (1830–1895), for example, is remembered only for EWING, sung to the words 'Jerusalem The Golden'. Sir Frederick Champneys (1848–1930), the writer of the tune ST JEROME, was an obstetrician by profession! Many other, more famous composers contributed to *Hymns Ancient and Modern*. They are too numerous to mention here, but most of the texts or tunes listed in the Glossary will be found in one or other edition of the book.

Arthur Sullivan

Denomination hymn books

Many other hymn books were produced in the nineteenth century as well as *Hymns Ancient and Modern*. Some were compiled especially for the use of particular church denominations. Reference has already been made to the early nineteenth-century revisions of the Wesleyan hymn books. Further revisions and new editions followed in the latter half of the century. A new Primitive Methodist Hymn Book appeared in 1886 (Supplement 1912), while the 'New Connexion' published *Hymns for Divine Worship* in 1864 to replace their earlier version of Charles Wesley's original 1780 compilation. In 1904, the Wesleyans and the New Connexion group came together to produce a new hymn book, the music edited by Sir Frederick Bridge, organist of Westminster Abbey. Hymn books were produced for the United Methodist Free Churches were issued in 1860 and 1889. The original *Bible Christian Hymn Book* was enlarged in 1838, being revised in 1860 and 1889. This last edition also included psalms and canticles.

The *Congregational Hymn and Tune Book* appeared in 1857 and 1862, thought to be the first collections which regularly placed the word 'Amen' at the end of every hymn text. The Congregationalists had originally produced a hymn book in 1836. This was revised in 1855, appearing with a supplement and (separate) tune book in 1859. The latter publication was entitled *The Bristol Tune Book*. A new collection, The *Congregational Church Hymnary*, was brought out in 1887, the music edited by Hopkins. A second book, with the music edited by Gauntlett, was privately printed in 1886 under the title *The Congregational Psalmist*.

In 1814, William Gadsby (1773–1844) published his *Selection Of Hymns For Public Worship* which proved popular in its later editions amongst the independent Calvinist baptists. The Baptist Church used their own collection *Psalms and Hymns* from 1858, although a music edition did not appear until 1900, when the title became *The Baptist Church Hymnal*. Charles Spurgeon (1834–1892) compiled his own hymn book in 1866 for his Baptist Congregation at his Metropolitan Tabernacle in London. *Church Praise* was the hymn book of the Presbyterian Church of England from 1885 for a few years. Thereafter this church used the same hymn books as the Scottish Presbyterians, *The*

Church Hymnary, also used by a number of other 'Free' Churches.

It was a mark of the influence of the Anglican Church in general and *Hymns Ancient and Modern* in particular that many of the Nonconformist hymn collections contained hymn texts and tunes which had either been used or rejected by Baker, Monk and their colleagues when compiling their collection, being in any case edited by men associated primarily with the Church of England, as noted above. If there was a difference between *Hymns A & M* and these other books it was that the editors of the former book and its later editions and supplements sought to exclude the more sensational or sentimental words and music.

Welsh tunes

Industrial Wales in the Victorian age, like the north of England, was dominated by the Nonconformist chapels. Both areas had strong traditions of singing and both stimulated the composition of many hymn texts and tunes. There can be very few hymn collections published since the middle of the nineteenth century which do not contain Welsh tunes, such as ABERYSTWYTH, CWM RHONDDA or HYFRYDOL.

Popular Gospel songs

The nineteenth century saw a revival of interest in hymns and hymn singing in the Roman Catholic Church. Much of the work of the Catholic hymn writers proved popular amongst the Anglo-Catholic wing of the Church of England. F.W. Faber

(1814–1863) and Edward Caswall (1814–1878) were the key figures in this respect. It is interesting to note that when their hymns appeared in Anglican and other Protestant hymn books the words were often changed to reflect a different theological approach. Faber founded the Oratory at Brompton in London, where he introduced simple and popular music as a means of aiding worship, just as his forbears in the Catholic Church had done centuries before him. The English Catholic Church also used many of the more popular gospel songs, as imported from America, in their worship, albeit at the service of Benediction, the only place where vernacular hymn texts could be sung until 1964. As with other denominations, the simple gospel-type music was popular in the missions to the poor of the country.

This kind of music was collected together in collections such as the *Mirfield Mission Hymn Book*, first published in 1907 (revised 1948) by the Community of the Resurrection at Mirfield, Yorkshire, an Anglican

The Village Choir rehearsing the Christmas anthem
(from Illustrated London News, December 1863)

religious house. As well as the hymn tunes and texts found in Anglican books, this and other similar collections include hymns such as 'What A Friend We Have In Jesus' and 'Count your Blessings'. Some of these 'mission hymns' even appeared in church hymn collections such as *The English Hymnal*, though they are labelled as being 'Not for ordinary use'.

Carols re-introduced

Carols were re-introduced into church worship in the nineteenth century. J.M. Neale (see above), together with Helmore, discovered many old carols through their researches into early folk music. Neale's editing of *Piae Cantiones* (referred to earlier in this book) also helped to stimulate carol singing. Many of the tunes from this collection, as translated and edited by Neale became popular, including 'Good King Wenceslas' and 'Unto Us A Boy Is Born'. Other English musicologists – notably Davies Gilbert and William Sandys – collected carols from the west country in the 1820s and 1830s. A number of collections were published, including, later in the century, *Christmas Carols New And Old* (1871), edited partly by John Stainer and regarded by many as almost a companion volume to *Hymns Ancient and Modern* and R. R. Chope's *Carols For Use In Church* (1875).

Stainer's collection, which he edited with H. R. Bramley, contained some forty-two pieces in its first edition. The 1878 revision added a further twenty eight and was reprinted many times. Chope's collection was revised in 1894, at which time 103 carols were added to the first edition's 112 pieces. Much of the music dated from Victorian times, but several of Orlando Gibbons' tunes originally published in George Wither's 1623 hymn book were also included. Some of the resurrected carol melodies became hymn tunes for texts which did not have a Christmas theme. One example of such an adaptation is the tune KINGSFOLD, often sung to the words 'I Heard The Voice Of Jesus Say, Come Unto Me And Rest'. It also appeared as a folk melody, often with seasonal texts attached.

Carol services

This interest in carols resulted not only in the inclusion of such music in both special anthologies and general hymn books, but also in the development of carol services, such as the 'Nine Lessons and Carols' made famous by King's College, Cambridge. The earliest such services were held in Truro Cathedral in the 1870s.

German chorales

The greatest of the German chorale texts and tunes had been written by the eighteenth century, though the influence of the chorale remained strong, both in Germany and abroad. Large numbers of tunes, along with their texts translated into other languages, appeared in many hymn books, including the great Victorian collections. Baron C. K. J. von Bunsen (1791–1860), the Prussian Ambassador in London was instrumental in persuading hymn book editors in Britain to translate the great

KINGSFOLD. (D. C. M.)
In moderate time ♩ = 80.
From an English Traditional Melody.

I HEARD the voice of Jesus say,
  'Come unto me and rest;
Lay down, thou weary one, lay down
  Thy head upon my breast':
I came to Jesus as I was,
  Weary, and worn, and sad;
I found in him a resting-place,
  And he has made me glad.

H. Bonar, 1808–89.

Kingsfold – tune and text

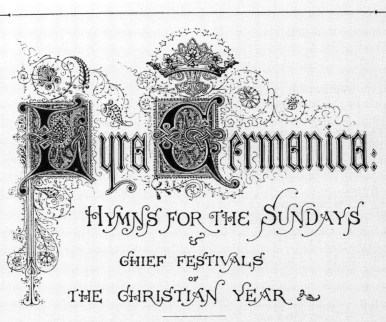

Lyra Germanica:

Hymns for the Sundays
&
Chief Festivals
of
The Christian Year

Translated *from the* German *by* Catherine Winkworth.

With Illustrations *by* John Leighton, F.S.A.
and others.

THIRD EDITION.

Cast thy bread upon the waters for thou shalt find it after many days.
Ecc. IX. I.

LONDON:
LONGMAN, GREEN, LONGMAN, ROBERTS, & GREEN.
1864.

Title page of 'Lyra Germanica', 1864

chorale texts as well as being a leading figure in the German movement for hymn book reform.

Catherine Winkworth (1829–1879) was one of the most prolific of the translators of German texts into English. Her *Lyra Germanica* was first published in 1855. Frances Elizabeth Cox (1812–1897) translated many such hymns, encouraged by Bunsen. Bunsen produced his own hymn book for the German Hospital at Dalston, London. This was based on his earlier German hymn book, first published in 1833.

The chorale style was also adopted by German song composers in the late eighteenth and nineteenth centuries. Peter Cornelius's song 'Three Kings', for example, has a chorale accompaniment – 'How Brightly Shines The Morning Star'. While German chorale tunes and texts have long proved popular in Britain and North America, the same cannot be said of hymns from the English-speaking world; few tunes or sets of words have been translated into German, for example – perhaps because there was already a well-established and richly diverse heritage of music and poetry for church worship.

American hymns

In North America, many people sang hymns at home as well as in church. Some of the hymn books used were based on European collections; others were compiled and produced in North America. Some of the American hymn tune composers were also singing teachers, who did much to improve performance standards in church, including teaching people to read music. A major force in this respect was Lowell Mason (1792–1872), whose work appeared in hymn books published on both sides of the Atlantic. Not only did the music sung in many of the American churches have to be simple, but the musical notation was to be easily read by a wide range of people. The use of different shapes to denote musical intervals became popular as a way of notating hymns – an alternative, in fact, to *tonic sol-fa*. The music was also based on popular folk styles of the period.

Shape-note music was sung at camp and 'revival' meetings – especially popular in rural communities from c1800 to the outbreak of the American Civil War. The hymns were so popular that they were often described as 'white spirituals'. Indeed, the music influenced the development of the negro spiritual and, indirectly, the rise of black American music in general and jazz in particular. Three hymn collections in particular were reprinted many times during the nineteenth century: *Songs of Sion* (1821), *Southern Harmony* (1835), and *Sacred Harp* (1844).

Towards the end of the nineteenth century, a number of other religious movements used the hymn as a way of spreading their particular brand of the Gospel message. The camp and revival songs referred to earlier resulted in the production of a compilation of what became known as 'mission hymns' because of the missionary zeal with which they were

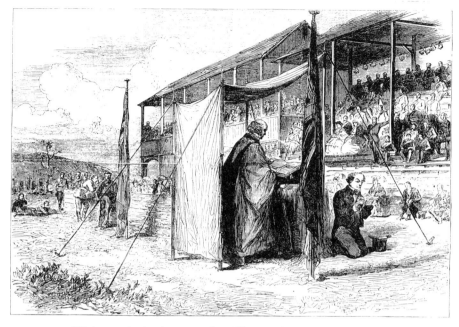

Divine service in the camp (from Illustrated London News, 1863)

produced and because of the role which they performed, much as earlier hymns had done.

Moody and Sankey collections

The American Evangelists Dwight L. Moody (1837–1899) and Ira D. Sankey (1840–1908) compiled and edited the best known collections. They became so popular that, like Tate and Brady and Sternhold and Hopkins before them, Moody and Sankey had the distinction of having their names used as shorthand for the hymn collections for which they were responsible. The music which they included in their collections was of a poor quality and little is now regularly performed. At the time of its appearance, however, Moody and Sankey's work did much to convert people of working class origins to Christianity. One contemporary writer said that they 'reduced the population of Hell by a million souls' thanks to their hymns.

A similar approach was adopted in Britain by William Booth, founder in 1878 of The Salvation Army. He adopted an approach which resulted in a style of hymn singing drawing on the popular tunes, harmonies and rhythms of Victorian popular music. In this he was following the tradition developed by the Wesley brothers and dating back to the time of Luther if not the early Christian preachers.

Moral songs

One other type of nineteenth-century hymnody deserves a mention. In 1862, the Church of England Total Abstinence Society was founded. Similar movements were formed in the Nonconformist churches. These 'temperance' groups were dedicated to reducing alcoholism amongst the working classes and a number of hymn collections were produced especially for them. Many of the texts in these collections were not hymns at all, but moral songs designed to shame the guilty (usually the father of the family) into repentance. 'Father, Dear Father, Come Home!' is a typical example.

For many years, there was a reaction against Victorian hymns and their tunes, discussed in this chapter. They were often regarded as over-sentimental, even by contemporary writers. Edwin George Monk (1819–1900), a church musician of the period, wrote:

A good tune, whether strong, or tender, or jubilant in its character, should possess something beyond mere vigour, or tenderness, or joy-fulness; it should be devout, unsecular, soul-stirring . . . Few only of the popular tunes now in use will answer to this description. Let us, therefore, dread the tendency to which I have

A service on the plantation (from Illustrated London News, 1863)

We shall Meet By and By.

"The ransomed of the Lord shall return and come to Zion with songs and everlasting joy upon their heads; they shall obtain joy and gladness, and sorrow and sighing shall flee away."
(ISAIAH XXXV. 10.)

REV. J. ATKINSON.   H. P. MAIN.

1. We shall meet be-yond the riv-er, By and by, By and by;
2. We shall strike the harps of glo-ry, By and by, By and by;

And the dark-ness shall be o-ver, By and by, By and by;
We shall sing re-demp-tion's sto-ry, By and by, By and by;

With the toil-some jour-ney done, And the glo-rious bat-tle won,
And the strains for ev-er-more Shall re-sound in sweet-ness o'er

We shall shine forth as the sun, By and by, By and by
Yon-der ev-er-last-ing shore, By and by, By and by.

3. We shall see and be like Jesus,
   By and by, by and by;
   Who a crown of life will give us,
   By and by, by and by;
   And the angels who fulfil
   All the mandates of His will
   Shall attend, and love us still,
   By and by, by and by.

4. There our tears shall all cease flowing,
   By and by, by and by;
   And with sweetest rapture knowing,
   By and by, by and by;
   All the blest ones, who have gone
   To the land of life and song,
   We with shoutings shall rejoin,
   By and by, by and by.

A tune from Moody & Sankey: Sacred Songs and Solos

alluded; and encourage in its stead, sober, broad, and elevating melodies, supported by masculine, church-like, and untheatrical harmonies'.

William Henry Monk (1823–1889), editor of *Hymns Ancient and Modern*, criticising the more 'sensational' tunes of the mission hymn books, said:
'It is not the pretty tune that is the most fit, nor the most popular that is the most worthy of popularity. Some of the melodies of Moody and Sankey . . . are popular enough – but it is quite another question whether they are worthy of associ-ation with God's worship. Are they and the hymns they accompany not rather the exponents of a somewhat unwholesome and sentimental feel-ing, too personal and effeminate for public worship?'

Whatever the answer to this ques-tion, there is no doubt that the nine-teenth century and the Victorian age produced the single largest group of hymns which are still regularly sung at church and secular gatherings throughout the world, whether it be the refined tunes of S.S. Wesley or the evangelising beat of Moody, San-key and others.

CHAPTER SIX

The Hymn Today

THERE is a story that when Percy Dearmer (1867–1936), a Canon of Westminster, went to see the composer Ralph Vaughan Williams (1872–1958) to ask him to compile a hymn book, he promised the musician that it would only take some two months and incur expenditure of approximately £5. It took two years and cost Vaughan Williams £250 out of his own pocket! Though an organist early in his career, Vaughan Williams felt that he knew too little about either church music or hymns to edit a book until Dearmer told him that if he refused to accept the offer the commission would be given to another (unnamed musician) whom the composer disliked intensely. The result was *The English Hymnal*, one of the best-known twentieth-century hymn books.

The revised edition of *Hymns Ancient and Modern* had been published in 1904, with a number of newly-published or commissioned hymn tunes from the leading church composers of their day, most notably C. H. H. Parry (1848–1918) and C. V. Stanford (1852–1924). This book had not proved popular (the original 1861 edition and its supplements and revisions had remained in use despite their supposed replacement by the 1904 edition). The *Daily Telegraph* had described the collection as 'a lamentable book – bad taste, bad poetry, bad theology'. The 'awful red book' as it was known, had disappointed those in the Anglican Communion – including Dearmer – who were of the Anglo-Catholic tradition. The initial intention was to compile a supplement to *Hymns Ancient and Modern* but Dearmer and his like-minded colleagues soon realised that it would be possible to

find enough material to fill a complete hymn book.

The English Hymnal

Dearmer had collected only hymn texts; Vaughan Williams had to find appropriate music. Along with Cecil Sharp (1859–1924), the folk dance and song expert who had nominated Vaughan Williams as the editor of *The English Hymnal*, the composer had already collected a good many tunes in his researches into English folk song. Many of these melodies were included in the new hymn book, often with harmonisations by Vaughan Williams himself. An example of such a tune is MONK'S GATE ('He who would valiant be'), so called after the place in Horsham where he first heard and recorded it. The collection included a number of what were described as 'French Church Melodies'; some were metrical arrangements of plainsong and

Ralph Vaughan Williams

others were new compositions. These 'melodies' were brought to Britain from France by the Reverend J.B. Croft. Vaughan Williams also asked his composer friends – notably Gustav Holst (1874–1934) to contribute tunes to the collection. The result was an anthology of the best possible texts and tunes, including many plainsong and chorale melodies – the latter often with harmonies by J.S. Bach.

Working on the Hymnal not only allowed Vaughan Williams an opportunity to use his work on folk song to good effect, but it also introduced the composer to much other church music. The THIRD MODE MELODY, hymn number 92 in the collection, inspired Vaughan Williams to write the *Fantasia on a Theme of Thomas Tallis*, a major contribution to the English orchestral repertoire, as well as some fifteen hymn tunes such as DOWN AMPNEY ('Come Down, O Love

Divine') and SINE NOMINE ('For All The Saints'). He also wrote a number of descants to other hymn tunes.

The English Hymnal proved to be a popular and well-used hymn book. The original intention had been for Mowbray's Publishing to produce the collection (Dearmer was a good friend of the person then responsible for the company) but Vaughan Williams insisted that Oxford University Press be the publishers. Agreement was reached that this should be the case only on condition that Mowbray's Publishing (who had been involved in the original idea) have their name on the title page as joint publishers, as is still the case.

Between its first publication in 1906 and its golden jubilee fifty years' later, it had sold over five million copies. It was well edited and relevant to the practical Christian philosophy of the many churches which used the collection. The music stressed the great and diverse musical heritage of the church and in its inclusion of traditional melodies reinforced the effectiveness of the age-old link between sacred and secular music as evinced in the hymn.

A second edition of *The English Hymnal* appeared in 1933. The plainsong hymns were revised in the light of changing views on their performance, notably influenced by the monks of Solesmes Abbey in France. Their free style of performing plainsong is well known world-wide. In 1962, The *English Hymnal Service Book* was published. This combined hymns from the parent book with Merbecke's communion music, the psalter and other parts of the service. Such a combination was similar to the seventeenth century practice of binding together the *Book Of Common Prayer* with Sternhold and Hopkins. The *Hymnal For Scotland* is a version of *The English Hymnal* which has been authorised for use in the Episcopal Church of Scotland. *English Praise*, a supplement to *The English Hymnal*, was published in 1975.

Improved standards

Other hymn collections appeared earlier in this century which aimed to improve both literary and musical standards. G.R. Woodward (1848–1934), a member of the Cowley Fathers' Community at Oxford, studied older hymnody in order to bring it into the modern repertory. He edited *Carols For Christmastide* (1892), *Carols For Easter And Ascensiontide* (1894), *The Cowley Carol Book* (1902/1919), *The Cambridge Carol Book*, *The Italian Carol Book* and *Songs Of Syon* (1904, revised 1910 and 1923). The latter collection concentrated on the Genevan and Germanic tunes and texts of the Reformation, while the carol collections were the first to include many texts and tunes which are now popular: 'This Joyful Eastertide' is perhaps the best example.

Robert Bridges (1844–1930), Poet Laureate, produced *The Yattendon Hymnal* together with H.E. Wooldridge (1845–1917) in 1899. Like Woodward, Bridges was concerned to improve literary standards in

hymn collections. His hymnal is named after the parish where he lived and into which he first introduced his book. Bridges transcribed Latin and other hymn texts into a modern English while maintaining a high standard poetically. He also aimed to match text and music in as sensitive a way as possible, while being aware of the fact that it was not always possible to match the accentuation of different verses of text to the one tune. For him, the 'enormous power that the tune has of enforcing or even creating a mood [was] the one invaluable thing of magnitude which overrules every other consideration'.

The texts of the *Yattendon Hymnal* were to reappear in a number of other collections, including *The English Hymnal*. The editors of the latter book were also concerned about the quality of the words and commissioned a number of new hymns from noted writers of the time such as G.K. Chesterton. The same was true of the limited circulation *Oxford Hymn Book*, first published in 1908. This was one of the first collections to include carols alongside hymns. Edited by Basil Harwood (1859–1949), organist of Christ Church Cathedral Oxford, the book shows his indebtedness to his tutor S.S. Wesley, being one of the main sources of the latter's hymn tunes.

Use in schools

Vaughan Williams edited the music for the hymn book *Songs Of Praise* and, with Percy Dearmer and Martin Shaw (1875–1958) *The Oxford Book of Carols*. Both collections proved popular. *Songs Of Praise*, first published in 1926 and enlarged in 1931, was used primarily in schools rather than churches, partly because of its non-denominational base and the need for a hymn book in the light of the 1944 Education Act which required some such act of worship in schools each day. Long regarded as the most complete anthology of its kind, the carol collection has only recently been superseded. *The BBC Hymn Book* was another inter-denominational book which was introduced to serve the daily broadcast service.

The Roman Catholic Church continued its interest in congregational singing. Richard Runciman Terry (1865–1938), first organist of Westminster Cathedral, edited *Calvin's First Psalter* and a modern edition of the *Scottish Psalter* of 1635 as well as the *Westminster Hymnal*. This latter collection was the first authorised Roman Catholic hymn book in Britain. First published in 1912, a second edition appeared in 1940 and a third in 1964. Since 1964, congregational music has played an important part in all the regular worship of the Roman Catholic Church and new hymn books have been produced to meet the demand.

Revised collections
The twentieth century has seen the revision of the many great hymn collections which are used throughout the world. *Hymns Ancient and Modern*, for example, was revised in 1950; *The English Hymnal* became *The New English Hymnal*; this new edition was published in 1986 by The Canterbury Press Norwich, an imprint owned by the publishers of its traditional rival in the Anglican Church, Hymns Ancient & Modern. The Baptist, Congregational and Methodist Churches all renewed or revised their hymn collections. These books have drawn on an ever broader range of music and texts, while at the same time omitting the poorer quality texts and tunes of which men like Bridges were so critical.

Whereas in previous ages congregations would be used to singing only a few different tunes or hymn texts, or not even singing in the church service at all, there is now a rich repertory to choose from, whether dating from the early Christian Church, the eighteenth century or the twentieth, or whether originating from the Continent, North America or Britain. In some cases, the hymn book editors have had too many tunes and texts to cope with! In the Preface to the 1900 edition of *The Baptist Hymnal*, for example, it was noted that the previous editions together contained over 1,600 hymns – too many for most congregations to contend with in a lifetime, let alone a year of churchgoing!

Supplements
In many cases, supplements have been produced which add new tunes and texts to existing hymn books. Reference has already been made to the additional hymn books which complement *Hymns Ancient and Modern Revised* and *Hymns and Songs*, a supplement to *The Methodist Hymn Book*, was published in 1965, for example. Alongside these collections are the 'mission' collections of groups

such as the Salvation Army and others, where Moody and Sankey still find a place, and the interdenominational books, including *Songs Of Praise* and *The BBC Hymn Book*.

As in earlier centuries, a return to evangelism in churches meant a renewal of interest in popular or folk music styles of the period. The Twentieth-Century Light Music Group, led by Geoffrey Beaumont (1905–1971), a member of the Community of the Resurrection at Mirfield, began to produce hymn tunes and texts which used a simple style designed to appeal to many ordinary people for whom the more traditional hymns would be of only limited interest.

Based on 'pop'

A similar approach was adopted by Sydney Carter (b. 1915), whose tunes are firmly based on folk and 'pop' music. His 'Lord Of The Dance' uses a North American 'Shaker' tune; yet another example of folk music finding its way into church, though in this case the original already had a religious pedigree. Malcolm Williamson (b 1931), Master of The Queen's Musick since 1975, has also written tunes in the 'light music' style. The criticism of much of this music is that it uses an idiom which to many people is already out of date. No doubt the best of the hymns will survive, adding to the repertory in the way that the outstanding work of previous generations has done.

Chil-dren, lift your voi - ces   On this hap-py morn.

TITLE.

COMPOSER, ETC.

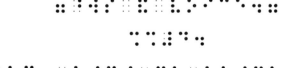

An example of a Braille hymn tune
(courtesy of the Royal National Institute for the Blind)

106

The twentieth century has been a period of ecumenism – a coming together of the different religious denominations in a way not seen before. The music of the different churches has overlapped more than ever before as a result. In 1929, for example, a joint Conference of the three branches of the Methodist Church then in existence was held to produce a new hymn book. The process of consultation included churches in other parts of the English-speaking world. The influence of Charles Wesley was still evident in the 1933 *Methodist Hymn Book* which resulted, though as with other hymn books and their twentieth-century revisions, a number of the Victorian favourites were omitted in favour of others 'which better express the same truths'. While the collection was still a *Methodist* one, the editors hoped that, like all the other major hymn books, it would be widely used. Psalms and 'Hymns for Little Children' were included and there was a wide range of texts and tunes which had originated from non-Wesleyan sources and periods.

Hymns and Songs, the 1965 supplement, took this a stage further with modern words and old tunes, old tunes and old words, modern tunes and modern words! Everything from a Calvinist psalm tune to a Sydney Carter hymn, or from an ancient verse to the words of a Lutheran chorale or a text by Fred Pratt Green (b1903), one of our most prolific modern hymn writers, is included. Negro spirituals and African texts have also become popular, even in 'established' churches.

The 1980s and early 1990s have seen the publication of a wide range of 'modern' hymn books which aim to revitalise hymn singing in the context of late twentieth-century musical, social and liturgical tastes. The Anglican, Catholic and Nonconformist Churches have all introduced new collections which aim to combine the best and most popular of the older tunes with new words and music which, it is felt, will be more relevant to today's church worshippers than the older Victorian hymns and collections. Many Roman Catholic churches now use *Hymns Old and New Revised* (1986), while the United Reformed Church published *Rejoice and Sing* in 1991. This collection maintains that church's commitment to psalm as well as hymn singing, as does the Methodist Church's 1983 book. The Baptist Church's latest hymn book, *Baptist Praise and Worship* (1991), includes many new hymns and worship songs as well as the best of the traditional repertoire. So does *Worship Songs Ancient and Modern*, published by The Canterbury Press Norwich, in 1992, as a means of 'bridging the gap' between the more traditional hymns and popular songs, while at the same time providing church musicians and congregations with music befitting the dignity of worship, primarily in the Church of England. Bearing in mind the need to provide for equality of worship, some hymn books are now being published which only use inclusive language in their texts, as for example *Hymns for Today's Church*. *Mission Praise* (1985) has proved to be one of the most popular of the latest

24 Everlasting love

CHILDREN

John Dankworth

1 Ev - er-last-ing Fa - ther, the Prince of Peace,
2 There's a new di - men - sion of love sub-lime,

Peacefully

born as Christ our Sav - iour, and shall we cease, now we are
far be-yond all ques - tion of space and time; out-side our

his, saved by his grace, prais-ing the name of Je - sus?
world, in-side our heart, mys-tery of grace and mer - cy:

*An example of a modern hymn tune by John Dankworth
and words by Paul Wigmore from 'Worship Songs Ancient and Modern'*

108

generation of hymn book, at least in Britain.

There are many other hymns books, too numerous to mention in a short guide such as this. What all these many publications demonstrate is that there are few, if any, signs of a diminution of interest in hymn singing or hymn writing. Age-old favourites are listed along with the most up-to-date 'popular' tune or contemporary text. One can find anything in a modern hymn book from an aboriginal melody to the DAMBUSTERS' MARCH, not forgetting the many monuments to hymnody from the time of the early church, through the Reformation and Martin Luther's work to the output of the Wesleys and the great nineteenth-century writers! These publications also show that the history and development of the hymn is, in a sense, the history of the church and also, to a certain extent, the history of popular music. As a means of bringing ordinary people together to worship God in music and poetry, the hymn in its various forms has no rival. The symbol of its success is as an enduring vehicle for huge congregations or small bands, professional musicians or the meanest amateurs. The hymn has stood the tests of time, fashion and theological change. Long may it remain so.

Noel Tredinnick conducts members of the choir and orchestra of All Souls, Langham Place, at the launch of 'Worship Songs' in St Margaret's, Westminster, 21 May 1992

109

Wenhaston Boys Choir (Suffolk), director Christopher Barnett, on tour at St Peter's, Rome, 1990.

GLOSSARY
of 100 hymns

The following is a representative selection of popular hymns through the ages, chosen from several sources, including favourites from many denominations and also taking into account the results of surveys carried out by programmes such as BBC TVs 'Songs of Praise'. Unfortunately, some favourites may have been omitted, but are nevertheless equally popular. It should also be remembered that many of these hymns are sung to other tunes.

Abide With Me
Words by Henry Frances Lyte (1793–1847); tune – Eventide – by William Henry Monk (1823–1889).
Probably written in 1847 – poem derived from 'Abide with us' (St Luke 24. 29). Tune composed and published with words in first edition of *Hymns Ancient & Modern* 1861.

All glory, laud, and honour
Words by Theodulph of Orleans (c.750 –c.821); tune – St Theodulph – by Melchior Teschner (1584–1635).
Written by Theodulph, supposedly whilst in prison, and translated by John Mason Neale (1818–1866). The tune was composed in 1615, and was used by Bach in his oratorio 'St John Passion'.

All people that on earth do dwell
Words – probably by William Kethe (?–c.1594); tune – Old 100th – composed or adapted by Louis Bourgeois (dates unknown).
Originally appeared in John Daye's *Psalter* (1560–1561). The tune was first associated with Psalm 134, but then set to Psalm 100, from which it derives its name.

All things bright and beautiful
Words by Mrs Cecil Frances Alexander (1818–1895); tune – Keats – by William Henry Monk (1823–1889).
A successful & popular hymn for children on the article of the Creed, 'Maker of Heaven & Earth'. First appeared in Mrs Alexander's *Hymns for Little Children* in 1848.

Alleluia! Sing to Jesus
Words by William Chatterton Dix (1837–1898); tune – Hyfrydol – by Rowland Huw Pritchard (1811–1887).
Much used during Ascensiontide, this hymn was written in 1866, and set with the tune (meaning Good Cheer) in the 1906 *English Hymnal*.

Amazing Grace
Words by John Newton (1725–1807); tune – Anonymous American folk-tune.
Although originally written in 1779 and set to the present tune much later, this hymn gained its popularity in the nineteen – sixties, being much used by the folk – singing fraternity.

And can it be that I should gain
Words by Charles Wesley (1707–1788); tune – Sagina – published by Thomas Campbell (dates unknown).
Containing many biblical references, suggestions that this hymn was written by John Wesley and was the Wesleys conversion hymn have been discounted.

And now, O Father, mindful of the love
Words by William Bright (1824–1901); tune – Unde et memores – by William H Monk (1823–1889).
Widely used Communion hymn, the name of the tune taken from the Latin form of a Communion prayer.

Angel voices, ever singing
Words by Francis Pott (1832–1909); tune – Angel Voices – by Edwin George Monk (1819–1900).

Both words and music were written for the opening and dedication of the organ of Winwick Church, Warrington, Lancashire.

As with gladness men of old
Words by William Chatterton Dix (1837–1898); tune – Dix – by Conrad Kocher (1786–1872).

Published as part of Dix's private collection originally. The tune was adapted by William Henry Monk (1823–1889) from a chorale by Kocher and despite the fact that Dix himself disapproved of it (*Companion to Hymns and Psalms* – Ed. Watson & Trickett – 1988), it's association with this hymn has persisted to this day.

Begin, my tongue, some heavenly theme
Words by Isaac Watts (1674–1748); tune – St Magnus – probably by Jeremiah Clarke (1673–1707).

First appeared in *Hymns & Spiritual Songs* (1707)-Watts speaks of God as Creator and Redeemer. The tune was named St Magnus in 1762, after the Church of St Magnus Martyr, London.

Behold, the mountain of the Lord
Scottish Paraphrases(1745 & 1781) altered; tune – Glasgow – T. Moore's *The Psalm Singer's Pocket Companion* (1756). The tune is named after the place where Moore's book was published.

Blessed assurance, Jesus is mine
Words by Frances Jane van Alstyne (1820–1915); tune – Blessed Assurance – Phoebe Palmer Knapp (1839–1908).

Mrs van Alstyne wrote the words after hearing the music of this hymn, and subsequently collaborated with Mrs Knapp in the writing of many more.

Born in song!
Words and music by Brian R. Hoare (1935–).

Written for a Wesleyan celebration in Sheffield in 1979, the tune is named after the house of the Dukes of Devonshire.

Breathe on me, breath of God
Words by Edwin Hatch (1835–1889); tune – Carlisle – by Charles Lockhart (1745–1815).

Although written in 1878, this meditative hymn was not used for public worship until 1886. The tune, also used for other hymns, was named after Holy Trinity Church, London – formerly Carlisle Chapel.

Christians, awake, salute the happy morn
Words by John Byrom (1692–1763); tune – Yorkshire – by John Wainwright (1723–1768).

Taken from a Christmas present poem, written by the author for his daughter; the tune should really be called Stockport – the place of birth and death of the composer.

Come down, O Love Divine
Words by Bianco da Siena (d.1434), translated by Richard Frederick Littledale (1833–1890); tune – Down Ampney – by Ralph Vaughan Williams (1872–1958).

Translated in 1867 from 13th century Italian 'Laudi', this hymn became popular once added to Vaughan Williams' tune (1906) which the composer named after his birthplace.

Come, Holy Ghost, our souls inspire
Words, 9th century, translated by Bishop John Cosin (1594–1672); tune – Veni Creator(Mechlin).

Cosin used his translation in his private devotions. Combined with the plainsong melody, it has a simple dignity all its own.

Dear Lord and Father of mankind
Words by John Greenleaf Whittier (1807–1892); tune – Repton – C Hubert H Parry (1848–1918).

Words from a poem; the tune is taken from Parry's oratorio 'Judith'.

For all the saints who from their labours rest

Words by William Walsham How (1823–1897); tune – Sine Nomine – by Ralph Vaughan Williams (1872–1958). Only eight of the original eleven verses are used today; the tune, composed for the words takes its name from the Latin meaning 'without a name'.

Forty days and forty nights

Words by George Smyttan (1822–1870); tune – Heinlein (Áus Der Tiefe) – probably by Martin Herbst (1654–1681).
The words were adapted by Francis Pott (1832–1909), and there have been many alterations to the text since, continuing to the present day. Originally thought to have been composed by Heinlein, the tune was first set to another hymn which included the words 'Aus der Tiefe' (out of the deep) in its text.

Give me joy in my heart, keep me praising

Anonymous; tune – Sing Hosanna – traditional.
Of uncertain origin; biblical references found in St Matthew.

Glorious things of thee are spoken

Words by John Newton (1725–1807); tune – Austria – by Franz Joseph Haydn (1732–1809).
Regarded by many as Newton's finest hymn. The tune was composed for the Austrian national hymn.

God be in my head

Book of Hours; tune – Walford Davies (1869–1941).
Anonymous words derived from a French verse and used in books of private devotions c. 1490. The tune was published in 1910 and has replaced all others

in the *Hymns Ancient & Modern New Standard* (1983).

God moves in a mysterious way

Words by William Cowper (1731–1800); tune – London New – from Scottish Psalter
Cowper wrote this hymn shortly before the nervous collapse in 1773, which dogged the latter years of his life. Despite this, the hymn speaks more of faith, hope and trust than of the eternal damnation which he so feared. The tune was changed to' London New' to distinguish it from another tune named' London' which appeared in the same publication in 1677, and was set to these words in *Hymns Ancient & Modern* (1861).

God of grace and God of glory

Words by Harry Fosdick (1878–1969); tune – Rhuddlan – Welsh traditional.
Written in 1930 to be sung at the opening service and dedication of the Riverside Church in New York City. The tune was set to the words in 1933.

God rest you merry, gentlemen

Words – traditional; tune – God rest you merry – English traditional melody.
The words were found in 1770, and the first printing of the melody was said to have been in 1796. Interesting in that the title can have two meanings depending upon where the comma is placed: 'God rest you, merry gentlemen' or 'God rest you merry, gentlemen' (in this context the word 'rest' means 'keep').

Good Christians all, rejoice and sing

Words by Cyril A Alington (1872–1955); tune – Vulpius (Gelobt Sei Gott).
The hymn was written specifically for the tune , Vulpius for *Songs of Praise* (1931). The tune is from Melchior Vulpius's 'Ein Schön geistlich Gesangbuch (1609).

Good King Wenceslas

Words by John Mason Neale (1818–1866); tune – unknown.

Wenceslas was a legendary king of Bohemia in the 10th century, who was famous for his generosity.

Great is thy faithfulness, O God my Father

Words by Thomas O. Chisholm (1866–1960); tune – Great is thy faithfulness – by William M. Runyan (1870–1957).

Written in 1923, in New Jersey and sent to Runyan to compose the music for them. First used by the Baptists in this country.

Guide me, O thou great Redeemer

Words by William Williams (1717–1791); tune – Cwm Rhondda – by John Hughes (1873–1932).

First written in Welsh, but later translated. Associated with this tune, it is much sung at rugby matches!

Hark the herald angels sing

Words by Charles Wesley (1707–1788); tune – Mendelssohn – adapted by Wiiliam H Cummings (1831–1915).

When originally written, each of the ten verses began with 'Hark, how all the welkin rings Glory to the King of kings'. Cummings adapted a chorus from 'Festgesang' – a cantata by Mendelssohn (1809–1847) composed to celebrate the invention of printing.

How sweet the name of Jesus sounds

Words by John Newton (1725–1807); tune – St Peter – by Alexander Robert Reinagle (1799–1877).

Called 'The Name of Jesus' in Olney Hymns (1779); the tune was named after the church where Reinagle was organist.

I heard the voice of Jesus say

Words by Horatius Bonar (1808–1889); tune – Kingsfold – English traditional.

Written at Kelso in the Scottish borders, when the author was minister there; published in 1846. The tune was arranged by Vaughan Williams (1872–1958) having heard the melody at Kingsfold, Sussex and thus named it.

I know that my Redeemer lives

Words by Samuel Medley (1738–1799); tune – Torquay – by William Youens (1833–1911).

Notable for its symmetrical text.

I to the hills will lift mine eyes

Scottish Psalter; tune – Dundee – Scottish Psalter.

A version of Psalm 121.

Immortal, invisible, God only wise

Words by Walter Chalmers Smith (1824–1908); tune – St Denio (Joanna) – Welsh hymn melody.

First printed together with this tune in 1906 in the *English Hymnal*. Earlier versions of the hymn had a comma after 'To all' at the beginning of the third verse, which actually makes more sense of the sentence.

In the bleak midwinter

Words by Christina G. Rossetti (1830–1894); tune – Cranham – Gustav Holst (1874–1934).

Said, in *Poetical Works* (1904) to have been written before 1872. and first used as a hymn in the *English Hymnal* (1906). Beautifully atmospheric, it combines with the music of Holst to give a haunting quality. The tune refers to a village near Holst's birthplace in Cheltenham.

It came upon the midnight clear

Words by Edmund H. Sears (1810–1876); tune – Noel – traditional English melody, adapted by Arthur S. Sullivan (1842–1900).

Written in Wayland, Massachusetts where the author was minister of the Unitarian Church, it bears a message which is true of all ages. Sullivan adapted the music from a Herefordshire folk-tune, and set it to the hymn in *Church Hymns* (1874).

Jerusalem the golden

Words by Bernard of Cluny, 12th century, translated by John Mason Neale (1818–1866); tune – Ewing – by Alexander Ewing (1830–1895).

Part of a poem by Cluny c. 1140, and translated by Neale in 1849. Ewing was an amateur musician who served as a Lieutenant Colonel in the Crimean War.

Jesus, good above all other

Words by John Mason Neale (1818–1866) – Verses 1 & 2, and Percy Dearmer (1867–1936) – Verses 3 & 4; tune – Quem Pastores Laudavere – adapted from a German MS of 1410.

Jesus lives! Thy terrors now

Words by Christian F Gellert (1715–1769); tune – St Albinus – by Henry J Gauntlett (1805–1876).

Translated from the German by Frances Elizabeth Cox (1812–1897), the hymn was originally called 'Easter Hymn'. The Alleluias were added to the tune when it was set to the words in 1861.

Jesus – the name high over all

Words by Charles Wesley (1707–1788); tune – Lydia – by Thomas Phillips (1735–1807).

From *Hymns & Sacred Poems* (1749) – there were originally 22 verses. The tune was attributed to T. Phillips although there is no evidence to suppport the fact. However, it is notable for having been mentioned in George Eliot's *Scenes from a Clerical Life* (c. 1857) and in Thomas Hardy's *The Return of the Native* (1878).

(*Companion to Hymns & Psalms* – Ed. Watson & Trickett – 1988).

Joy to the world, the Lord is come

Words by Isaac Watts (1674–1748); tune – Antioch – mostly from W. Holford's 'Voce di Melodia' (c. 1834).

Words translated from the last five verses of Psalm 98; used much at Advent, but more in America than in England, although now becoming more popular particularly with Baptists and Methodists.

King of Glory, King of Peace

Words by George Herbert (1593–1633); tune – Gwalchmai – by Joseph David Jones (1827–1870).

Originally from *The Temple* (1633) entitled 'Praise II'. It is not known whether the tune refers to a village near Llangefni in Anglesey, Wales, or to a 12th century Welsh bard.

Kum Ba Ya, my Lord, kum ba ya

Words – Anonymous; tune – Kum Ba Ya – traditional.

Of uncertain origin – Kum Ba Ya is thought to be pidgin English for 'Come by here'. The words and music have always been associated with each other, the music being described in *New Catholic Hymnal* (1971) as an African Spiritual.

Lead us, heavenly Father, lead us

Words by James Edmeston (1791–1867); tune – Mannheim – adapted from Friedrich Filitz (1804–1876).

The three verses signify the Trinity – Father, Saviour & Spirit, and were united with the music in 1875. Popularised for marriage services by its use at the weddings of the Princess Royal in 1922, and the future King George VI & Queen Elizabeth in 1923.

Let all mortal flesh keep silence

Words by Gerard Moultrie (1829–1885) from the Liturgy of St James; tune – Picardy – traditional French carol.

Based on a prayer from the Liturgy (4th century), Moultrie's translation appeared in 1864, the tune adapted by Vaughan Williams in 1906.

Let all the world in every corner sing

Words by George Herbert (1593–1633); tune – Luckington – by Basil Harwood (1859–1949).

The words are from *The Temple* (1633) a posthumous collection of poems by Herbert, and are antiphonal in structure. The tune is named after a village in Wiltshire.

Let us with a gladsome mind

Words by John Milton (1608–1674); tune – Monkland – by John Antes (1740–1811).

There are indications that Milton wrote these words at the age of fifteen. The tune was either composed or adapted by Antes, and originally set to Henry Baker's hymn 'Praise , O praise our God and King'. Monkland is the name of the village where Baker was vicar.

Love divine, all loves excelling

Words by Charles Wesley (1707–1788); tune – Love Divine – by John Stainer (1840–1901).

First published in *Hymns for those that seek, and those that have Redemption in the Blood of Jesus Christ* (1747); it is included in many hymn books of all English-speaking countries, and ranks with the best of the author's work. The tune was set in 1875.

Make me a channel of your peace

Words – based on a traditional prayer; tune – Channel of Peace – Sebastian Temple (1928 –).

Based on a prayed supposedly by St Francis; the present arrangement of words and music are both by Temple – a member of the Los Angeles Franciscan Community.

Mine eyes have seen the glory of the coming of the Lord

Words by Julia Ward Howe (1819–1910); tune – Battle Hymn – attributed to William Steffe (unknown).

Written in 1861, six months after the outbreak of the American Civil War, after Mrs Howe had heard troops singing 'John Brown's Body'. Entitled 'The Battle Hymn of the Republic' in the February 1862 edition of the *Atlantic Monthly*, and sung to the tune 'Glory, Hallelujah', although no claims to the composition of this tune can be supported.

Morning has broken

Words by Eleanor Farjeon (1881–1965); tune – Bunessan – Gaelic melody.

Percy Dearmer (1867–1936) asked Eleanor Farjeon to write some words for the tune, to be included in *Songs of Praise* (1931).

My heart and voice I raise

Words by Benjamin Rhodes (1743–1815); tune – Ascalon – from Silesian Folk Songs.

This hymn, very popular in Methodist churches, has many biblical references to Creation, Redemption and the coming of the kingdom. The tune was used by Franz Liszt (1811–1886) in his oratorio 'The Legend of St Elisabeth' in 1862.

Now thank we all our God

Words by Martin Rinkart (1586–1649); tune – Nun Danket – by Johann Crger (1598–1662).

Written in Saxony during the Thirty Years War, a great hymn of praise and thanksgiving. Bach used the chorale in one of his organ preludes and two of his Cantatas (192 & 79).

Now the day is over

Words and tune (Eudoxia) by Sabine Baring-Gould (1834–1924).

Printed in the *Church Times* in 1865, this

hymn has become common in all English-speaking countries. It is much used as an evening hymn for children.

O come all ye faithful
Words (18th century) translated by Frederick Oakley (1802–1880); tune – Adeste Fideles – probably by John Frances Wade (1710/11–1786).
Latin words first written down by Wade, with the music in 1750. Commonly called the 'Portuguese Hymn', but reasons for this differ.

O come, O come, Emmanuel
Words – 18th century, translated by John Mason Neale (1818–1866); tune – Veni Emmanuel – anonymous.
Based on the seven antiphons sung at Vespers before Christmas, the tune is essentially plainsong.

O God, our help in ages past
Words by Isaac Watts (1674–1748); tune – St Anne – probably by William Croft (1678–1727).
Considered by Julian in his *Dictionary of Hymnology* (1892) to be one of Watts' finest compositions, the words inspire hope and stability. Croft was organist at St Anne's, Soho, from 1700–1712.

O Jesus, I have promised
Words by John E. Bode (1816–1874); tune – Thornbury – by Basil Harwood (1859–1949).
A very popular confirmation hymn, sung to many tunes as well as the above.

O Love that will not let me go
Words by George Matheson (1842–1906); tune – St Margaret – by Albert Lister Peace (1844–1912).
The author wrote of the hymn : ' It was composed with extreme rapidity: it seemed to me that its construction occupied only a few minutes, and I felt myself rather in the position of one who was being dictated to than of an original artist. I was suffering from extreme mental distress, and the hymn was the fruit of the pain' (Julian – *Dictionary of Hymnology*, 1892). The tune was composed specifically for the hymn which has such an unusual metre, and is named after Margaret, Queen of Scotland.

Once in royal David's city
Words by Mrs Cecil Frances Alexander (1818–1895); tune – Irby – by Henry J Gauntlett (1805–1876).
Frequently used as a processional hymn at Christmas time.

Onward, Christian soldiers
Words by Sabine Baring-Gould (1834–1924); tune – St Gertrude – by Arthur S Sullivan (1842–1900).
Written for a Children's Festival in 1864, this is a fine example of the Church Militant. The tune was specifically composed and named after a friend of the composer's.

Praise, my soul, the King of heaven
Words by Henry Frances Lyte (1793–1847); tune – Praise my soul – by John Goss (1800–1880).
The tune was composed for the hymn which takes its text from Psalm 103.

Praise to the Holiest in the height
Words by John Henry Newman (1801–1890); tune – Richmond – by Thomas Haweis (1734–1820).
From Newman's poem *The Dream of Gerontius*. Also sung to the tune – Gerontius by John B Dykes (1823–1876).

Rock of Ages, cleft for me
Words by Augustus Montague Toplady (1740–1778); tune – Petra – by Richard Redhead (1820–1901).
Four lines of this hymn were published in 1775 in the *Gospel Magazine*, and the rest appeared in the following year. Toplady was the editor of the magazine.

The tune was published in 1853, and given the name Petra (rock) in 1861.

Ride on, ride on in majesty

Words by Henry H Milman (1791–1868); tune – Winchester New – adapted by William H Havergal (1793–1870).

Julian, in his *Dictionary of Hymnology* (1892) describes this as 'the most popular hymn for Palm Sunday in the English language'. The tune is from 'Musikalisch Handbuch (Hamburg, 1690), and is also often associated with the hymn 'On Jordan's bank the Baptist's cry'.

Saviour, again to thy dear name we raise

Words by John Ellerton (1826–1893); tune – Ellers – by Edward John Hopkins (1818–1901).

The words could be used by all people as a daily hymn. The tune, originally composed to be sung in unison, was later adapted for four parts.

Seek ye first the kingdom of God

Words and tune by Karen Lafferty (unknown).

Written in the early nineteen seventies and often sung as a round – particularly popular among youth groups.

Silent night, holy night

Words by Joseph Mohr (1792–1848); tune – Stille Nacht – by Franz Grüber (1787–1863).

Written by Joseph Mohr, who was assistant priest at the church of St Nicholas in Oberndorf, Austria, he handed it to the acting organist – Grüber – when the organ broke down on Christmas Eve, 1818, and asked him to set it to music for guitar – there being one available at the time. It was performed that same evening by two solo voices with guitar since when its popularity has remained undaunted.

Sing, my tongue, the glorious battle

Words by Venantius Fortunatus (c.535–c.600); tune – Pange Lingua – plainsong melody in the Phrygian mode.

A hymn of selected verses translated by Percy Dearmer (1867–1936).

Soldiers of Christ, arise

Words by Charles Wesley (1707–1788); tune – St Ethelwald – by William Henry Monk (1823–1889).

Another strong example of the church militant.

Take my life, and let it be

Words by Frances R Havergal (1836–1879); tune – Consecration – by William H Havergal (1793–1870).

Frances Havergal was a fervent evangelical, strongly born out by the dedication of these words. The tune, originally called Patmos, was composed by her father, although not specifically for this hymn, but it was the family's wish that they be used together.

Teach me, my God and King

Words by George Herbert (1593–1633); tune – Sandys – from Sandys' *Christmas Carols*, 1833.

Frequently used in school assemblies, although many of the children probably sang the verses over the years without really understanding their meaning.

Tell out, my soul, the greatness of the Lord

Words by Timothy Dudley Smith (1926 –); tune – Woodlands – by Walter Greatorex (1877–1949).

A very popular modern hymn based on St Luke 1.46–55, in the *New English Bible*. The tune, set to these words in 1969, was named after one of the houses at Gresham's School, Holt, Norfolk.

The church's one foundation

Words by Samuel J Stone (1839–1900); tune – Aurelia – by Samuel S Wesley (1810–1876).

Written in 1866 signifying the traditional view of the church, the tune was named by Wesley's wife. The hymn was used as the processional at Canterbury Cathedral, Westminster Abbey, and St Paul's Cathedral for the Bishops assemblies of the 1888 Lambeth Conference.

The day thou gavest, Lord, is ended

Words by John Ellerton (1826–1893); tune – St Clement – by Clement C Scholefield (1839–1904).

This hymn became popular after it was used at services of thanksgiving for Queen Victoria's Diamond Jubilee in 1897.

The first nowell

Words – anonymous; tune – The First Nowell – English traditional.

Variously arranged in both hymnals and carol books, and often sung with descant.

The God of love my Shepherd is

Words by George Herbert (1593–1633); tune – University – by Charles Collignon (1725–1785).

A paraphrase of Psalm 23, the tune refers to Cambridge University where Collignon was a Professor of Anatomy.

The King of Love my Shepherd is

Words by Henry Williams Baker (1821–1877); tune – Dominus Regit Me – by John Bacchus Dykes (1823–1876).

Yet another version of Psalm 23, for which the tune was specifically composed.

The Lord's my Shepherd, I'll not want

Words – Scottish Psalter; tune – Crimond – probably by Jessie Irvine (1836–1887).

Jessie Irvine's father was the minister of Crimond, Grampian. The hymn became a firm favourite after its use at the wedding of Princess Elizabeth in Westminster Abbey (1947), and in St Paul's Cathedral at the silver wedding anniversary of King George VI and Queen Elizabeth (1948).

The strife is o'er, the battle done

Words – 17th century, translated by Francis Pott (1832–1909); tune – Victory – by William Henry Monk (1823–1889).

Slightly differing versions appear in several hymnbooks, some with 'Alleluia's' at the beginning. The first three lines of the tune were adapted from a 'Gloria Patri' by G.P. Da Palestrina (1525–1594), the final 'Alleluya's' were composed by Monk.

There is a green hill far away

Words by Mrs Cecil Frances Alexander (1818–1895); tune – Horsley – by William Horsley (1774–1858).

Based upon the words: 'suffered under Pontius Pilate, was crucified, dead and buried' from the Apostles Creed. Exceedingly popular hymn intended for children and widely used. Note the double use of the word 'dearly' in the last verse, meaning both affectionately, and at such great cost to himself.

Thine be the glory, risen, conquering Son

Words by Edmond L Budry (1854–1932); tune – Maccabaeus – George F Handel (1685–1759).

Translated into English in 1923 by Richard B Hoyle (1875–1939), and made popular in Britain by the Methodists, it has always been sung to this tune, which comes from the chorus 'See, the conquering hero comes' in Handel's oratorio 'Judas Maccabaeus'.

Thou didst leave Thy throne

Words by Emily E S Elliot (1836–1897); tune – Margaret – by Timothy Matthews (1826–1910).

Sometimes sung with varied refrain, although originally written to be sung identically after each verse; the tune was composed for the words in 1876 and has remained the only one in use ever since.

Thou God of truth and love

Words by Charles Wesley (1707–1788); tune – St Godric – by John Bacchus Dykes (1823–1876).

Originally a love poem written for his future wife, Sarah Gwynne, and adjusted by John Wesley for public use; the tune refers to a 12th century saint.

Thou whose almighty word

Words by John Marriot (1780–1825); tune – Moscow – by Felice de Giardini (1716–1796).

Despite its inclusion in most hymn books, the words, based on the Trinity are rarely printed identically, although differences are usually slight. The composer died in Moscow, hence the name of the tune.

Through all the changing scenes of life

Words by Nahum Tate (1652–1715) & Nicholas Brady (1659–1726); tune – Wiltshire – by George Thomas Smart (1776–1867).

Paraphrased from Psalm 34, but present day version shorter than the original. The tune was first set to this hymn in 1863.

To God be the glory, great things he has done

Words by Mrs Frances J van Alstyne (1820–1915); tune – To God be the glory – by William H Doane (1832–1915).

An evangelical favourite, popularized by Sankey (1840–1908) and much used by Methodists and Baptists.

We shall overcome

Words possibly by Albert Tindley (unknown).

The original hymn from which these words seem to be derived appeared in *New Songs of the Gospel* (published in 1900). The first 4 bars of the tune are very similar to the hymn 'O Sanctissima'. The hymn became the unofficial hymn of the Negro civil rights movement.

We plough the fields and scatter

Words by Matthias Claudius (1740–1815) and translated by Jane M Campbell (1817–1878); tune – Wir Pflügen – by Johann A.P. Schülz (1747–1800).

When originally published in 1782, this hymn was 17 stanzas long, and was a description of a harvest thanksgiving. The tune was set to these words in 1861 (C S Bere – 'Garland of Song').

When all thy mercies, O my God

Words by Joseph Addison (1672–1719); tune – Contemplation – by Frederick A Gore Ouseley (1825–1889).

Originally written with 13 verses, different hymn books use different selections from these. The tune was written for the hymn in 1889.

When I survey the wondrous cross

Words by Isaac Watts (1674–1748); tune – Rockingham – by Edward Miller (1735–1807).

Watts obviously considered this to be a Communion hymn, as it appeared in the third book of *Spiritual Songs and Psalms* under the general heading 'Prepared for the Holy Ordinance of the Lord's Supper. The tune was named after the Marquis of Rockingham, twice Prime Minister of Britain and a friend of Miller's.

When we walk with the Lord

Words by John H Sammis 1846–1919); tune – Trust and Obey – by Daniel B Towner (1850–1919).

According to *Companion to Hymns & Psalms* (Methodist Publishing House Ed. Watson & Trickett), this hymn was written after an incident during one of Moody's meetings in Massachusetts c. 1886, when a young man stood up and said that he felt unsure but was going to trust and obey. Towner told Sammis, who wrote the words. Words and tune have been used together ever since.

While shepherds watched their flocks by night

Words by Nahum Tate (1652–1715); tune – Winchester Old – by Thomas Este (1540–1608).
Taken from St Luke 2. 8–14, the tune first appeared in Este's *The Whole Booke of Psalmes*, and the name Winchester not until 1621 in Ravenscroft's *The Whole Booke of Psalmes*.

Who would true valour see

Words by John Bunyan (1628–1688); tune – Monk's Gate – by Ralph Vaughan Williams (1872–1958).
From *The Pilgrim's Progress*, many still prefer the original version, complete with its 'goblins and foul fiends', despite the fact that Percy Dearmer (1867–1936) wrote an alternative version beginning 'He who would valiant be'. The tune was adapted by Vaughan Williams from a folk-song he heard sung in Monk's Gate, Sussex.

With gladness we worship, rejoice as we sing

Words by George Rawson (1807–1889); tune – Datchet – by George J Elvey (1816–1893).
Popular mainly with Methodists, the hymn first appeared in 1876, but was not set to this tune until 1933. Datchet is a town near Windsor, Elvey having been organist at St George's Chapel from 1835–1882.

Ye choirs of new Jerusalem

Words by Fulbert of Chartres (c.960–1028); tune – St Fulbert – by Henry J Gauntlett (1805–1876).
Translated from the Latin by Robert Campbell (1814–1868), the tune was set to the hymn in 1861 and named after the author.

Ye holy angels bright

Words by Richard Baxter (1615–1691); tune – Darwall's 148th – by John Darwall (1731–1789).
The hymn was written to the tune of Psalm 148, as found in Sternhold and Hopkins's 'Old Version'.

Index of Tunes

*Massed choirs at the Royal Albert Hall for the Jubilee Festival of
the Royal School of Church Music on 25 June 1987*

DISCOGRAPHY

The following list is a representative sample of choral recordings currently available. The name of the recording company is given, followed by the disc or cassette number. The first number refers to the compact disc recording and the second (in italics) to the cassette. Where only one number appears, this refers to the compact disc, unless in italics, in which case the recording is available on cassette only.

Famous Hymns of Praise
Choir of St Mary's Episcopal Cathedral, Edinburgh
Dir. Dennis Townhill;
Organ: Peter Backhouse
Priory Digital PRCD 376

English Choral Music
The Choir of Gloucester Cathedral
Dir. John Sanders;
Organ: Mark Blatchley
Priory Digital PRCD 218; *PRC 218*

Choral Evensong from Hereford Cathedral
The Choir of Hereford Cathedral
Dir. Roy Massey
Priory Digital PRCD 247; *PRC 247*

Choral Evensong from Truro Cathedral
The Choir of Truro Cathedral
Dir. David Briggs
Priory Digital PRCD 322; *PRC 322*

Evensong for St Cuthbert's Day
The Choir of Durham Cathedral
Dir. James Lancelot
Priory Digital PRCD 296; *PRC 296*

Choral Music of Charles V Stanford
The Choir of Chichester Cathedral
Dir. Alan Thurlow
Priory Digital PRCD 312; *PRC 312*

Great Cathedral Anthems
The Choir of Guildford Cathedral
Dir. Andrew Millington
Priory Digital PRCD 257; *PRC 257*

Great Cathedral Anthems – II
The Choir of Norwich Cathedral
Dir. Michael Nicholas
Priory Digital PRCD 351; *PRC 351*

Music for Holy Communion
The Choir of Wakefield Cathedral
Priory Digital PRCD 341; *PRC 341*

Music for Passiontide
The Choir of Wells Cathedral
Priory Digital PRCD 362; *PRC 362*

Choral Music of Bairstow
The Choir of York Minster
Priory Digital PRCD 365; *PRC 365*

Famous Hymns of Praise
The Choir of St Mary's Cathedral, Edinburgh
Priory Digital PRCD 371; *PRC 371*

The Complete Psalms of David:
Volume 1. 'Hear My Prayer O Lord'
The Choir of Hereford Cathedral
Dir. Roy Massey
Priory Digital PRCD 290; *PRC 290*

Volume 2. 'O Praise The Lord Of Heaven'
The Choir of Wells Cathedral
Dir. Anthony Crossland
Priory Digital PRCD 337; *PRC 337*

Volume 3. 'The Earth Is The Lord's'
The Choir of Durham Cathedral
Dir. James Lancelot
Priory Digital PRCD 343; *PRC 343*

Volume 4. 'In Jewry Is God Known'
The Choir of Lichfield Cathedral
Dir. Jonathan Rees-Williams
Priory Digital PRCD 383; *PRC 383*

Volume 5. 'Praise The Lord Ye Servants'
The Choir of Gloucester Cathedral
Dir. John Sanders

Priory Digital PRCD 387; *PRC 387*

Volume 6. 'The Lord Is My Light And Salvation'
The Choir of Guildford Cathedral
Dir. Andrew Millington
Priory Digital PRCD 416; *PRC 416*

Volume 7. 'Let God Arise'
The Choir of Norwich Cathedral
Dir. Michael Nicholas
Priory Digital PRCD 409; *PRC 409*

Volume 8. (To Be Released)
The Choir of Ely Cathedral

Volume 9. (To Be Released)
The Choir of Rochester Cathedral

Volume 10. (To Be Released)
The Choir of York Minster

Carols from Clare
Clare College, Cambridge, Choir and Orchestra
John Rutter
Electrical & Mechanical Industries
CDM7 69950–2; *EG 769950–4*

The Holly & the Ivy (Carols)
Clare College, Cambridge
John Rutter
Decca 425 500–2; *425 500–4*

Festival of Lessons & Carols (1979)
King's College, Cambridge, Choir
Philip Ledger
Electrical & Mechanical Industries
CDM7 63180–2; *EG 763180–4*

Procession with Carols on Advent Sunday
King's College, Cambridge, Choir
Philip Ledger
Electrical & Mechanical Industries
CDM7 63181–2; *EG 763181–4*

On Christmas Night
York Minster Choir
Francis Jackson (Organ)

Chandos CHAN 6520; *MBTD 6520*

Music from the Eton Choirbook
The Sixteen
Harry Christophers
Meridian CDE 84175; *KE 77175*

The World of King's
King's College, Cambridge, Choir
Sir David Willcocks
Decca 430 092–2; *430 092–4*

Carols from King's
King's College, Cambridge, Choir
Sir David Willcocks
Classics for Pleasure
CD-CFP 4586; *TC-CFP 4586*

Christmas Music from King's
King's College, Cambridge, Choir
Sir David Willcocks
Electrical & Mechanical Industries
CDM7 64130–2; *EG 764130–4*

Christmas Carols from King's College
King's College, Cambridge, Choir
Willcocks and Philip Ledger
Electrical & Mechanical Industries
CDM7 63179–2; *EG 763179–4*

The Psalms of David, Volume 1
King's College, Cambridge, Choir
Willcocks
Electrical & Mechanical Industries
CDM7 63100–2; *EG 763100–4*

The Psalms of David, Volume 2
King's College, Cambridge, Choir
Willcocks
Electrical & Mechanical Industries
CDM7 63101–2; *EG 763101–4*

The Psalms of David, Volume 3
King's College, Cambridge, Choir
Willcocks
Electrical & Mechanical Industries
CDM7 63102–2; *EG 763102–4*

Anthems for the Chapel Royal, Purcell
Trinity College Choir, Cambridge
Dir. Richard Marlow
Conifer CDCF 152; *MCFC 152*

The Six Motets, Bach
Trinity College Choir, Cambridge
Dir. Richard Marlow
Conifer CDCF 158; *MCFC 158*

Carols for Today
Canterbury Cathedral Choir
Dir. Wicks
Conifer CDCF 160; *MCFC 160*

Sacred Choral Music, Walton
Trinity College Choir, Cambridge
Dir. Richard Marlow
Conifer CDCF 164; *MCFC 164*

Psalms of David, Schütz
Trinity College Choir, Cambridge
Dir. Richard Marlow
Conifer CDCF 190; *MCFC 190*

Psalms, Sweelinck
Trinity College Choir, Cambridge
Dir. Richard Marlow
Conifer CDCF 205; *MCFC 205*

Come, Holy Ghost, Choral Evensong for Whitsuntide
Trinity College Choir, Cambridge
Dir. Richard Marlow
Conifer CDCF 207; *MCFC 207*

Carols from Trinity
Trinity College Choir, Cambridge
Dir. Richard Marlow
Conifer CDCF 501; *MCFC 501*

Classic Hymns
CBSO Chorus, CBSO Brass Ensemble
Peter King, Simon Halsey
Conifer CDCF 502; *MCFC 502*

Glorious Trinity
Choir of Trinity College, Cambridge
Dir. Richard Marlow
Conifer CDCF 503; *MCFC 503*

Thine be the Glory, Hymns for all seasons
Seaford College Chapel Choir
Dir. Philip Hill, David Bell (Organ)
Conifer CDCF 511; *MCFC 511*

And the following from The Canterbury Press Norwich:

**Hymns Ancient & Modern New Standard
No. 1: 20 Lent, Holy Week and Easter hymns**
The Choir of Portsmouth Cathedral
Dir. Anthony Froggatt
HAC 841

No. 2: Selection of 18 hymns from Hymns for Today
Singers from Royal School of Church Music
Dir. Lionel Dakers
HAC 851

No. 3: 18 hymns for Advent, Christmas and Epiphany
The Choir of Canterbury Cathedral
Dir. Allan Wicks
HAC 861

New English Hymnal
18 hymns for the Christian Year and Rite A: A New English Folk Mass
RSCM Nicholson Singers
Dir. Michael Fleming.
Organist: Andrew Fletcher
HAC 872

Worship Songs Ancient & Modern
Selection of 23 songs
Choir and musicians of the Langham Singers,
conducted by Noel Tredinnick:
St Albans Singers conducted by Barry Rose:
and Millmead Church Guildford Group led by Jonathan Veira available on cassette (LANG C 006) and compact disc (LANG D 006) & distributed through Word (UK) on the Langham label.

127

The Moscow Orthodox Church Male Choir
(They held their UK premiere performance on 25 September 1993,
in East Anglia, promoted by Wingfield Arts)

BIBLIOGRAPHY

Much has been written about hymns and hymn singing. The text refers to the major hymn books and similar collections published over the centuries and the interested reader is encouraged to look at these and to review their content and approach. The following list of titles is intended as a brief guide to those requiring further information on the main topics covered in this study.

CHURCH MUSIC IN GENERAL
Archbishop's Commission on Church Music, *Report: In Tune with Heaven*, London: Hodder & Stoughton, 1992.

Blume, Friedrich, *Protestant Church Music: A History*, London: Victor Gollancz, 1975.

Caldwell, John, *The Oxford History of English Music* Vol 1, Oxford: Oxford University Press, 1975.

Dakers, L., *Parish Music*, 3rd. ed., Norwich: The Canterbury Press Norwich, 1991.

Davidson, J. *A Dictionary of Protestant Church Music*, New Jersey: Scarecrow Press, 1975.

Gatens, William, *Victorian Cathedral Music in Theory and Practice*, Cambridge: Cambridge University Press, 1986.

Long, Kenneth, *The Music of the English Church*, London: Hodder & Stoughton, 1972.

Rhys, Stephen and Palmer, King, *ABC of Church Music*, London: Hodder & Stoughton, 1967.

Routley, Erik, *A Short History of English Church Music*, London: Mowbray, 1977.

Temperley, Nicholas, *The Music of the English Parish Church*, Cambridge: Cambridge University Press, 1979.

THE HYMN
Bradley, Ian, *The Penguin Book of Hymns*, Harmondsworth: Penguin, 1990.

Braley, Bernard, *Hymn Writers*, 3 volumes, London: Stainer & Bell, 1987–1991.

Diehl, Katharine, *Hymns and Tunes: An Index*, New Jersey: Scarecrow Press, 1966.

Drain, Susan, *The Anglican Church in Nineteenth-Century Britain: Hymns Ancient and Modern, 1860–1875*, (Lampeter): Edwin Mellen Press, 1989.

Frost, Maurice, *Historical Companion to Hymns Ancient and Modern*, London: Clowes, 1962 [now published by The Canterbury Press Norwich].

Houghton, Elsie, *Christian Hymn Writers*, Bridgend: Evangelical Press of Wales, 1982.

Julian, John, *A Dictionary of Hymnology: Setting Forth the Origin and History of Christian Hymns of all Ages and Nations*. First Published 1892; Reprint Edition, New York: Dover, 1957. Later edition in four volumes, New York: Gordon Press, 1977.

Kaan, Fred, *Hymn Texts*, London: Stainer & Bell, 1985.

Leaver, Robin, with Morgan, Paul, *English Hymns and Hymn Books: Catalogue of an Exhibition held in the Bodleian Library, Oxford*, Oxford: The Library, 1981.

Lowther-Clarke, W., *A Hundred Years of Hymns Ancient and Modern*, London: Clowes, 1960.

Manning, Bernard, *Hymns of Wesley And Watts*, London: Epworth Press, 1988.

Manwaring, Randle, *A Study of Hymn-Writing and Hymn-Singing in the Christian Church*, [Lampeter]: Edwin Mellen Press, 1991.

Messenger, R. and Pfatteicher, H., *A Short Bibliography For The Study Of Hymns*, New York: Hymn Society Of America, 1964.

Perry, David, *Hymns and Tunes Indexed: By First Lines, Tune Names and Metres* , Croydon: Hymn Society/Royal School of Church Music, 1980.

Reynolds, William, *A Survey of Christian Hymnody*, New York: Holt, Rinehart & Winston, 1963.

Routley, Erik, *The Music of Christian Hymnody*, London: Independent Press, 1957.

Routley, Erik, *The Musical Wesleys*. London: Jenkins, 1968.

Tamke, Susan, *Make a Joyful Noise Unto The Lord: Hymns As a Reflection of Victorian Social Attitudes* , Athens: Ohio University Press, 1978.

Tennyson, G., *Victorian Devotional Poetry*, Cambridge, Mass.: Harvard University Press, 1981.

Watson, Richard, Trickett, Kenneth, *et.al.*, *Companion to Hymns and Psalms*, Peterborough: Methodist Publishing House, 1988.
(A number of books like those by Frost and Watson/Trickett have also been produced as companions to specific hymn books; details are given in the bibliographies of the works listed above)

THE CAROL

Greene, Richard L., *The Early English Carols*, Revised edition, Oxford: Oxford University Press, 1977.

Keyte, Hugh and Parrott, Andrew, *The New Oxford Book of Carols*, Oxford: Oxford University Press, 1992.

Routley, Erik, *The English Carol*, London: Herbert Jenkins, 1958.

THE PSALMS

Leaver, Robin, *Goostly Psalmes And Spirituall Songes: English and Dutch Metrical Psalms from Coverdale to Utenhove, 1535–66*, Oxford: Oxford University Press, 1991.

Zim, Rivka, *English Metrical Psalms: Poetry as Praise and Prayer, 1535–1601*, Cambridge: Cambridge University Press, 1987.

THE ORGAN

Baker, David, *The Organ: A Brief Guide . . .*, Princes Risborough: Shire, 2nd edition, 1993.

Edson, Jean S., *Organ Preludes: An Index to Compositions on Hymn Tunes, Chorales, Plainsong Melodies, Gregorian Tunes and Carols*, New Jersey: Scarecrow Press, 1970.

Langwill, Lyndesay G. and Boston, Noel, *Church and Chamber Barrel Organs*, Edinburgh: Langwill, 1979.

Thistlethwaite, Nicholas, *The Making of the Victorian Organ*, Cambridge: Cambridge University Press, 1990.

INDEX

Note the index covers only the main text and not the glossary, index of tunes, discography or bibliography. Italicised entries denote collections of hymns, psalms or prayers. Italicised page numbers denote a relevant illustration.